How to be open to God's miracles

*Joyce,
I pray you be opened.
Always in His Name,
Trisha Mounce*

Trisha Mounce

Copyright ©2023 *Trisha Mounce*

All Rights Reserved

Dedication

To the one who saved me

Jesus Christ.

Acknowledgments

Second only to God my husband Michael is the reason I have completed this book and I am blessed to be experiencing this life with him. Michael thank you from the bottom of my heart for allowing me to follow my God driven desire to share my story. Your support has been immeasurable. Without your continued encouragement and belief in my abilities this book would never have come to pass. I love you with every part of my being. Thank you!

Mom, you have always prayed for me when I needed it the most. That coverage of Jesus's blood over my life has brought me to where I am today. You have always shown me the importance of having Christian values. Words cannot begin to express the gratitude I have for being raised by a mother such as yourself. From the bottom of my heart thank you for everything you have done to bring me to this place of pure Joy in Jesus.

My three children Brayden, Emily and Allyson without the three of you I would lack content that has made my life story all that much more invaluable. From the depths of my soul, you are my legacy and I love you all with every part of my being.

Brian Hopkins, thank you for losing control of your tow truck that rainy day on June 4th 2019. With every breath of my being I need you to understand the joy that has come from the pain of that day. The suffering that we struggled through together will always be a bond we share. You are truly a good man and I consider myself fortunate to have ran into you.

Brian Nieves, with your skill and knowledge my mind was opened to possibilities I never thought possible. You are a true testament to 1 Thessalonians 5:11 "So encourage others and build each other up, just as you are already doing." Thank you for all you have done to coach me into a new walk with Christ.

As we age we can look back on times in our lives and see God at work through people whom have encouraged us and shown us the love of Jesus Christ. These to follow are just a few of the many I'd like to give credit and gracious thanksgiving.

> Dana Linhoff- my podcast friend who put up with me through times I didn't deserve it. Bless you my dear friend

> Jason Gaszak- my present pastor- Roots Church Saint Clair MO

> Bobbi Dunn- my spiritual mother who was instrumental in my walk with Christ from a young age (meet me at the gates dear friend)

> Tonya & Larry Kelso- my group leaders whose prayers led me to take leaps of faith I never thought possible.

> Everyone in my Roots Church Group who prayed this book into completion you are all loved and appreciated beyond words.

About the Author

Trisha Mounce served honorably in the United States Navy. She is known for her service to others through her past volunteer work in areas of her passion, the mental health sector and in the pro-life community. After 25 years of working as a self-employed real estate appraiser and raising her three children she took her biggest leap of faith. She is presently serving others by following God's plan in her life. She is sharing her story of faith and hope in Jesus's name by using her gift of entertaining with humor and her talkative nature as a writer and public speaker.

Introduction

The purpose of this book is for me to follow God's purpose in my life. If you're laying your eyes on these words know I am humbled and gracious to God for the infinite possibilities this book has for you and your life as it has been a profound journey for me to have written it.

Though these words and those to follow are written by me I have drawn great resources from the Lord and have at times felt as I wrote some by hand that it wasn't my hand doing the writing but that the words were Spirit written. I must admit a little bit scary at times as I felt like I had even zoned out a bit to come back to the paper with more writing that I remembered. I attribute it to the closeness one can experience to Christ when you engulf yourself in Him. The closeness that comes with taking your control off the table and allowing God full access to your life. My leap of faith if you will.

My family and I, we are known to speak in movie and song quotes and a friend of mine (V) once advised me to write my book just like I talk. With that being said I hope you take pleasure in the various connections I make throughout this book and find them enlightening to what could be considered a tough topic to start off as a writer. Yes, that is right you are holding in your hands the beginning of my leap of faith in a no control zone trusting God with everything lifestyle I never expected. But Hallelujah He has me here today.

When I decided to do the three sections, Me, God, and You I pondered the thought of what it might look like to the reader that I am starting the book with me instead of God. I came to this realization that my story isn't what is most important within this book and that the meat is in the middle. You and I are just the bun. And buns are porous, the meat is the juicy goodness that is God. We need to soak it all up. My deepest apologies to any vegetarians or vegans.

My hope and prayer for you is that as your eyes scan the words written on these pages to come that you experience a deep opening of your heart and soul to the miracles God performed in my life and that of which He desires to show you in yours. My heart is full of gratitude to Jesus Christ for my life and for this opportunity to share how He changed everything for me. From the depths of my soul Thank You for taking time to experience EPHPHATHA.

Contents

Dedication i

Acknowledgments ii

About the Author iv

Introduction v

ME

CHAPTER 1 - My Miracle(s) 1

CHAPTER 2 - Guardian Angels 12

CHAPTER 3 - GRATITUDE 20

GOD

CHAPTER 4 - No Such Thing as KARMA 35

CHAPTER 5 - Miracles 51

CHAPTER 6 - Spirit-Filled Peace 71

CHAPTER 7 - Confidence Comes with Christ 85

CHAPTER 8 - Feeling God's Presence 100

YOU

CHAPTER 9 - Who Am I To Be Used 114

CHAPTER 10 - Awaken Your Soul 125

CHAPTER 11 - CALL TO ACTION!!! 137

References 147

ME

CHAPTER 1

My Miracle(s)

The Game Changer

June 4, 2019. A day that will forever be etched in my life as the day God performed a miracle in my life that was beyond comprehension for me at the time and still astounds me to this day. That date marks a change in my life and an awakening that I never saw coming and will never forget.

My family and I live in a rural area, and that is the way we like it. There are no stoplights, rolling cow-covered countrysides, or bubbling creeks, and the nearest gas station is seven miles away. At night, you can walk outside and appreciate the magnitude of God's awesomeness as the stars shine brighter out here. Part of the enjoyment of living in this rural area is the enjoyable drive home every day. If you are a naturalist of any kind, you can appreciate the beauty of where I live, no hustle and bustle, just tranquility. My tree-covered street with American flags on every electric pole in itself is worth the drive to the rural Midwest. Living in the Midwest we get all seasons, and the changing of those trees throughout the seasons is majestic. I was grateful for my God-given picturesque drive. It was and still is today an enjoyable, relaxing, almost like a wind down from my driving all day, though I am still driving kind of drive.

Though I do a lot of driving, I rarely spend my time checking out the scenery. There are many times I see things I've never seen before while riding shotgun, though I have passed by those places many times. I find that I spend most of my time while driving, staring at the road directly in front of me. "A slave to the asphalt grind" I once heard my father describing it. When I would turn on our rural two-lane highway, more times than not, it changed, and my eyes would relax and divert a bit more from the road to gander at the glory. I don't know if I'd call it prideful in a bad way, but I was proud of where we were. I loved our middle-of-nowhere place. I was grateful to be where I was. As beautiful as the drive is, there is something else along the drive as a constant reminder, and that is all the crosses that pepper the curvy 2-lane highway that represents all the lives that have been lost on that stretch between my home and town.

It was roughly 6 pm. I had been on the road all day and was anxious to get home with the Saint Louis Bread Company in my car for my hungry family who were waiting for me. It had just started to mist and rain a bit as I turned off the main highway onto our curvy highway. I am not a slow driver. I am not even a slow driver today. I was very much ready to get home for the evening, and though I wasn't pedal to the metal, I was definitely speeding. There are not a lot of straightaways on this highway, but right before Calvey Creek Bridge, there is this awesome stretch of road where you can really let it fly. Everyone who drives this highway knows that no matter how fast you're flying on that stretch, the sharp curve right over the bridge requires a decrease in speed to make it safely around the bend. As I cleared the small bridge, I spotted through my misty windshield a bright red tow truck losing control and heading straight for me. The back end of the 2-ton truck was in my lane. I immediately stood on the brake with as much strength as I could muster to try and decrease my speed for the inevitable impact.

When I close my eyes even today, I can still see the rear of that truck and hear the sound of the metal crunching up around me. A lot from this point is spotty for me. Upon impact, it was like the tow truck's rear end was a bat to my SUV baseball. I was shot back and to the right, somehow missing every tree and electric pole. I came to rest at the bottom of a 12ft ravine amidst brush and debris while the tow truck spun around, coming to a stop just above me on the road, only feet from coming down upon the top of me in the ravine. Let me try to paint the picture of this a little bit better. When both vehicles were at a standstill, my car was 12 feet down in a deep culvert, and if you looked straight up from my windshield, Brian's front bumper was visible. Fifty miles an hour, and God stopped that 2-ton truck just in the nick of time with the only small curb on the rural road from ending both of our lives that day.

The hot blood in my left eye was blinding. It was so hot, where was I? I felt glass in my skin. It was hard to breathe; the pressure on my chest reminded me of when my sweet granddaughter Amara would sit on my chest and bounce up and down. Where was Amara? Was she in the back seat? Was I alone? I reached for my phone that just so happened to still be sitting on my lap after the 50mph impact, and dialed my boyfriend. It took 3 times of calling and in all honesty, I have zero memory of that. However, it was relayed to me after the fact. He was showering at the time, anxiously awaiting his dinner. The dinner was now splattered all over the windshield, the front seat, and the passenger floorboard. Later, I would hear a funny story about my daughter's friend Natalee (whom we all called Weenie) who was with her on the scene of the accident, and she asked if the broccoli cheddar soup that was everywhere was my vomit.

When my boyfriend Michael answered the phone, I remember screaming at him. I do not remember much of what I said, but from the stories I have heard, it must have been frightening and terrifying to hear. I recall claiming my eminent death. At that moment, I was certain I was going to die. I have always had a dark sense of humor. I've repeatedly over the years joked that I always assumed as much driving as I did and as fast as I drive that I knew I would meet my untimely death in a car accident. Here it was, my time was up, my ticket had been punched, I had lived my life, and it was check-out time. I would like to say that as a Christian, I've always had the disposition that I was okay with dying, that it was part of life, and that I wouldn't be afraid to die because I knew where I was going. Well, was I strong and courageous at that very moment when I thought I was going to die.... NO WAY? I was terrified and more afraid than I had ever been in my entire life. It is actually frustrating to recollect that fear, realizing that I was more afraid than when my daughter was in a car accident and I was rushing to her side. More afraid than when I lost that same daughter at Disney World. More afraid than any other time in my recollection. It was and is to this day, without a doubt, a fear I cannot even put into words. A fear so excruciating and tormenting that I do not believe my recollection of all the events that day will ever return to me. And to be honest, I am very thankful for that. Though, yes, my inquisitive mind would love to know the play-by-play of every little thing. I do understand why so much of the trauma is not recallable.

My family and I have an app on our phones called Life 360. My youngest daughter, who had just turned 16 less than a month prior was home. Michael yelled to her that I was in an accident not far from home and to get to me. She hopped in a vehicle ahead of him as he quickly threw on his clothes all while I continued my screaming on the phone. Thankfully for him, I was not always coherent. I remember looking down at my right shin and seeing the most vibrant white bone protruding from my skin, surrounded by what resembled a waterfall of crimson blood. It's one of the few true memories I have that's not been tainted by other's recollections. I would later find out that the bone protruding from my leg was that of many breaks; the word shattered was used to describe my tibia and fibular bones in my right leg. Today, my fibula is still in pieces. Turns out, since it's not a weight-bearing bone, it is no biggie. I can only assume that the break happened because I tensed so much when I saw the rear end of the town truck in my lane as I rounded the sharp corner to the left.

My head required stitching due to the impact of my head hitting the window. I would later learn that the traumatic injury to my brain would be my biggest area of contention. I couldn't breathe, as I would later learn was due to my broken sternum. Something I consider a blessing in disguise since I was never a big seat belt wearing. I am now, of course, but I wasn't back then. I rarely wore a seat belt because I drive so much, and I find it to be uncomfortable, but that day, I chose to put it on because of the misty rain. Something just told me to put it on. God obviously.

One of God's many miracles, I believe with all my heart that day, was that the tow truck was going to be in an accident whether I was there to stop him or not. Had the driver made it to the creek bridge, his life would have, with most certainty, been lost or seriously injured. Retrospect is a great thing when we can see the grace of God after the fact.

I would love to say in my time of fear, I remember a sense of calm or peace coming over me, and the skies opened, and God's glorious light shined down upon me, and I knew all was well. I am not mocking those who have had those God moments. That just did not happen to me. I did not see God at that very moment, though He was most definitely there, He was all over that situation, not just in the ravine or in the many people that were there to save me that day, but He did show himself in SO many ways throughout my experience as far back as months prior to my accident. He was preparing me and my family in so many ways. Ways I will explain further in this book. However, I am beyond blessed for His hands on my life that day.

I would later find out that the tow truck had several service concerns and shouldn't have been driven that day, or should it have, God's greater picture was being played out before my eyes in the form of a bright red 2-ton Dodge Ram tow truck.

I will never forget the look on Michael's face when he arrived on the scene before the paramedics opened the passenger door. I've never seen that look before, and I pray I never do it again. I believe what was most traumatic for my young daughter and Michael at the time was when the paramedics had to remove me from my car. Fortunately for me, I have zero recollection of this, but I have been told my screams were something that they will never forget. It took six paramedics to pull me out and up the steep ravine. Three men on both sides of me dragging me up the hill like pallbearers at a funeral. The ambulance sped off to get me to the hospital while my family followed behind, attempting to keep pace with the ambulance against the paramedics advice.

Celeste the Volvo

My desire for a Volvo was derived from when my family briefly lived in the Blue Ridge Mountains in a little town called Boone, NC. My father worked for a condo developer in the early 80's, and we moved quite a bit as my father established new construction condos, selling a percentage of a development, and then we'd move onto a new town. I hated Boone. I had moved from the comfort of being super popular in an area I still call home today, and I was angry. We were certainly not wealthy, but in Boone, we lived well. Not nearly as well as the uppity super popular 4th grade girl Georgia. Everyone wanted to be like her. While most of us were putting chains around the tires of our lightweight plastic cars, her mother drove a tank that required no chains. It was a four-wheel drive beast. She was getting to school on the days us middle-class kids were staying home. Her mother drove a Volvo. What kind of Volvo, I have no idea! All I know today is that it was cool, and I wanted one. I told myself when I had finally arrived at adulthood or achieved my financial worth, I'd be driving a Volvo.

My kids and I take great pleasure in naming our vehicles because, as a real estate appraiser driving roughly 50k miles a year, our family vehicles are part of our family. A true member of our family. It only seemed fitting that when I finally got my first Volvo she would be named Georgia. When I sat on those fancy leather heat-your-bum seats, I knew I had made it. I had arrived. My second Volvo, though not directly after Georgia, was named G2 in yet another homage to my 4th grade idol. Georgia, whom I ended up, became close to and greatly enjoyed her friendship for the short stent we made in what I can now say was a beautiful time in my childhood.

Celeste, she was my 3rd Volvo. She was a shiny, sparkly silver like a celestial being. She was an XC60—a smaller version of Georgia and G2, which were both larger XC90's. My kids were fond of the larger version only because of the third-row options, so I could cart around more of their friends. Celeste was my pride and joy.

After losing my job as a staff appraiser for Bank of America in 2011, I fell victim to being overextended and a poor steward of my money. I filed for bankruptcy in 2013. Therefore, I'd been at the mercy for some years of driving one hooptie after the next. Not that I didn't have some amazing memories with my children in Betty, our Chevy Avalanche, or that Nina the Nissan didn't come through in a pinch. They were both full of glorious memories and constant reminders of my financial failures as not only were they, not Volvo's, they were ridiculously high-interest debts that I was never going to pay off before they fell apart. Keeping in mind the 50k miles a year I was driving.

Celeste was my recovery car. She was more than just a car to me. She was a sign of recovery from financial struggles. She gave me a feeling of being back, whereas as a child, I had always felt I needed to be. More importantly, she, through God's Grace, was going to save my life.

When I purchased Celeste, I was prideful. I'll admit it. I was proud of my achievement. I gave no credit to God for getting me there. I felt as if I did it all on my own. I purchased a monthly car wash service and washed her several times a week. I considered it my relaxation time. Just me and Celeste. I'd hand dry her myself, taking my sweet time making sure I got every crevice dry and buffed. When I scrapped up her bumper on a street sign (a typical causality of my job), I cried out. Tears ran down my cheeks as I belted out various cuss words. This was how much value I had put into my car. How little did I know that only 3 months later, my most trusty companion was going to encompass me in all of her eight airbags as I sat at the bottom of a twelve-foot-deep ravine covered in my own blood and her glass stuck in my scalp, screaming to the two strangers that I would later call my guardian angels. I'll share more about my guardian angels later.

I purchased Celeste in November 2018, our heavenly time together ended on June 4th, 2019. Eight months I'd owned her. Dan, the owner of O&F Auto, someone in our small town I'd say who knows cars, said one day after my accident said to me, "That car saved your life!" After several comments like this I believed that she truly did, and I miss her. But there was a bigger picture. She served as a cage for God to reach down and protect me from death. He knew from the day He planned for me that I would buy my Volvo when I did. He knew that there was no way I'd survive being catapulted back like a baseball hit by a Saint Louis Cardinal in Larry the Laredo. He knew at the speed both Brian, the tow truck driver, and I were driving in the pouring rain that I wasn't going to be able to tell this story to you now in Larry. However, I had idolized my car, not God. Though I had put so much of my extra time into relaxing with Celeste instead of seeking Him. He saved me. God saw my sin in my worshipping her and praising my achievements and loved me even though and spared me that day. Why I ask? If not to share His love for you and for me.

According to NHTSA (National Highway Traffic Safety Administration) Celeste had a 5/5-star safety rating. Volvo's have a notorious reputation for having superb safety features. My heart says that Celeste was just that, my celestial being, my angel sent from God, and there isn't anyone who could possibly tell me anything different.

While in the dealership waiting for the salesman to purchase my 4th Volvo, I burst into tears. My feelings were so powerful I couldn't put them into words. I'm struggling even now with the emotions that were running through me. I was alive, and I was being blessed by God yet again. Everything had changed in my life because of the gift of Celeste. I had not deserved her, and I didn't feel like I deserved this one I was to purchase either. I didn't feel worthy. God opened my eyes to the way I had behaved with Celeste and still wanted me to be blessed with another.

Less than six months after my accident, I sat at a funeral for a godly man who was a family man who didn't deserve to die in a tragic car accident due to inclement weather like mine. I struggled a great deal with why he was taken and not me. This was something I found myself asking all the time. Why God, why did I deserve to live, and he didn't? Some of you are probably saying, "Who are we to question God's plan?". Oh, my dear friends, I've preached that more times than I care to admit. I can hear my mother's voice when I think of it, saying, "Don't you trust God, Trisha?" You can preach it, but it is not as easy to live it. When you feel you are facing/faced death, and you are saved, it is hard not to ask God those difficult questions. Survivors guilt is a real thing, and I believe it is only natural to wonder. I do not think He does not want us to ask. I believe He wants to show us. Though curiosity might have killed the cat, my curious mind drew me into His loving embrace with a closeness to Jesus unlike anything I had ever experienced before.

He wants us to always come to Him for everything. We all know it is easier to praise Him when all is well. I am learning to be more of a yay God person. Not the woe is me, where are you God, or why would you let this happen to me. Funny since I have asked God more times than I could count, "Why me?" since my accident. Truly, though, I have most often than not reached out my arms to Him when I was in the ravines, bleeding for His guidance. Sometimes, it takes that significant of a jolt for me. Fearing death is certainly a great way to get me to open my stubborn eyes to my God, who has been loving me and watching over me even when I was not deserving. What a HUGE realization it was for me to continuously see how something so simple as a car accident, something that happens daily in our world that He cared. God was there. He was protecting me. He cares about the little things. God does not only care about big catastrophic events in our world. He cares about me, little ole me. In the grand scheme of things, am I some great contributor to the world? That remains to be seen but God's ability is limitless. I have realized through this experience that who am I to inhibit God's work in and through me.

Getting Home

After what my mother was told should be a 2-hour surgery, that turned into a 5-hour surgery. I spent two weeks in the hospital, though it should have been longer. I was determined not to stay another day after two weeks. I did everything in my power to get out of there to start my true recovery from home. The hardest part of leaving the hospital was getting in the vehicle. Yes, it was painful and required a lot of shifting around, but that's not what I am talking about.

I was terrified to drive anywhere with anyone. It was my livelihood. Driving is what I did. How was I to overcome something so terrifying? I joked around with the doctors that I'd like to be teleported home and would require everyone to come to me for follow-ups. The first time I was in the car practicing in the parking lot prior to leaving was nothing short of excruciating. I was drugged up on so many anti-anxiety meds just to get in a car at that point, but I knew I needed to get past my fears. I refused to be defined by my accident.

To get home, we took the long way, not passing by my accident site. I remember pushing my right tattered and throbbing leg on the passenger side floorboard as hard as I could, as if to push on the brakes as I did on the game-changing day with almost every brake usage from Michael.

After I made it home at the encouragement of my family we drove by the crash site. As the adrenaline coursed through me, my heart beat out of my chest. My family joined me in my initial drive past the crash site. They offered ample details as tears streamed down my cheeks when I saw the remnants of my time in that deep culvert. I can still be caught tearing up even today from time to time when I pass by that spot. Not every time, thank the Lord. It does get better; there have even been a few times I've passed by and not even looked or thought about my time there. There are still those times when I with great gratitude, cry out to God with sincere thanksgiving for saving me that day. As time has passed, I still decrease my speed on that curve to a bit over a crawl, and thankfully, my entire family respects that curve and slows down for my benefit as if the likelihood of having another accident in the exact same place is even a statistical possibility.

Years later now, I find that red trucks coming at me on a curve still brings back memories and a tension within my body. Those feelings are Satan attempting to steal my joy of all the amazing things that happened from that impact that misty day in early June. Satan cannot have my gratitude to God for saving me that day. When those feelings of anxiety arise, I cover them up quickly with the true blood that saved me, Jesus Christ.

CHAPTER 2

Guardian Angels

Jesse & Marcus

There are certain times in our lives when something catastrophic happened, and we can recall where we were, what we were doing, and who we were with. One moment that comes to my recollection is 9/11. I was in a classroom taking a refresher course for my real estate appraiser's license. The lady in the office came running into my classroom of about a dozen, including the teacher, screaming and crying. After her brief explanation, we all went into her tiny office, sat around on the floor, and watched a shoebox-sized black and white TV for what seemed like hours. As the same visuals played over and over, we all sat in such shock that no one said a word. I remember thinking how could I bring my new unborn baby into this kind of chaotic world. I was 8 months pregnant with my daughter, who was born one month to the day after 9/11. I remember, for some reason, reading Psalms 91:11 it read, *"For he will order his angels to protect you wherever you go."* I took some solace in knowing God had angels there that day with each one who had lost their lives and/or their loved ones. I did not know anyone who had died or had been directly affected by 9/11, but I was mortified for all who had lost loved ones on that day. I know that Psalms 91:11 was true in my life when angels saved me in that ravine.

No matter where I have been in my spiritual journey, whether I was a fully devoted follower of Christ or floundering in my spiritual walk, I have believed in angels. I have, at points in my life, physically and spiritually, felt the overwhelming peace and calm of having what I felt was my terribly busy guarding guardian angel's presence.

My daughter Allyson, who had been present at the scene of my accident, claimed her belief in my guardian angels when she shared with me about the stranger who had just been there when she got there. My assumption was the scene was a little frightful for her, and there was a lot going on, but she said she had no idea where he had come from and how he had gotten there, but he was just there. We wrestled around with the possibility that maybe he was a passenger in the tow truck because Brian the driver, was sitting on the ground with his head between his hands in pain. I do not remember anyone being there, but the story that unfolded after the fact was beyond amazing. While I was in rehabilitation, she went to my car to get my personal affects out for me and was shocked to see a belt buckle in the front seat with the name Scott on it. A friend of hers had recently passed away in a freak wave runner accident named Scotty so of course, it was an emotional find for her and her friend Brittany, who had joined her in retrieving my belongings. She quickly brought it to my attention, and we set out to find out more about my guardian angel. As this angel had taken off his belt to tourniquet my leg to stop the bleeding and left his personalized belt buckle. Something I would soon find out was more than just a belt buckle.

I decided to put information on Facebook to get more details. I put a photo of my accident of which my daughter had taken as she stood at the top of the embankment looking down on my car in the ditch. The photo included whom I could only have assumed at that point was Scott's head showing up over the top of my car and, of course, a photo of Scott's belt buckle. I'm not a huge fan of social media, though I do enjoy the occasional info on how my high school buddies are doing or what my kids might be up to. I try not to invest too much of my time in endless scanning of everyone's thoughts. This time was so different; within less than 30 minutes, I had the name of the TWO young gentlemen who would never consider themselves angels, just being in the right place at the right time, they would later say. Doing the right thing would be these humble gentlemen's take on that day. But I digress their story is not even remotely done yet.

Jesse was the man in the photo with his head popping over the top of my shattered Celeste. He was Brian's son-in-law. Once Brian came to his senses, he too, made a phone call to his daughter Victoria. She quickly reached out to her husband, who just happened to be at his buddy's house, Marcus (more on him in a second), which was literally maybe a quarter of a mile from where Brian perched over me in his totaled tow truck. Jesse embodied the perfect example of someone who started his day expecting to end it one way on that day on which we met, but his day ended with him being dubbed my guardian angel for sure. A perfect example of someone who didn't need to be appreciated for "doing the right thing and was happy to have helped". He would later tell me. He was a perfect example of someone who might not have had a clue what to do in an emergency like this, but his innate instincts kicked in, and he said and did all the right things to help me in what I was still certain was going to be my untimely death.

You see, as young as I can remember, I always knew or assumed I would die in a car accident. Like my father before me, who (to clarify) did not die in a car accident, but he also had that same feeling. As he felt he would not make it past 30, I had given myself a little longer. I envisioned closer to 40. Here I was 46, well past my expected death age, so I certainly felt the end was near. Let me just say, Praise God that we do not know how and when we are going to die as we are living our lives and that only He knows that. Jesse was that day what I dubbed him as my "good ole boy angel". I will forever be grateful for his kindness, his support, and his quick thinking that most likely kept me from bleeding to death that rainy Tuesday evening.

Now, the belt buckle. I bet you have been wondering about that manly belt buckle with the name Scott on it, aren't you. Well, I sure was as soon as I determined that my two guardian angels were Jesse and Marcus. This is where God does amazing things, and it is important to the story. Probably more than even you and I will ever really know. You see the belt buckle? Well, that was Marcus's. He was wearing it at the time. He took off his belt and gave it to Jesse so he would be able to stop the surging blood at least partially from my gapping compound fracture. The belt buckle was Marcus's dad's buckle. It was very sentimental to Marcus as his father and mother had recently passed away. They were both killed in a car accident. Yes, you read that right. This young man had recently lost both of his parents in a head-on collision, and here he was without any concern for himself, handing over what I can only assume was a prize possession to an absolute stranger.

Marcus's parents, Scott and Nancy, were driving home one evening just as I was at 7:45 pm on November 23, 2015. On what appears to have been a similar two-lane highway like, Brian and I collided. I learned from a family friend that Marcus was even on the phone with his mother at the time of the accident, and he quickly rushed to the scene of the accident to find out that they had both suffered injuries that killed them immediately. Scott had been doing something that many of us do on our back road and that was he passed a slower-moving vehicle, probably just as anxious to get home as I was when his Chevy Malibu swerved into the northbound lane as both vehicles crested a small hill and Scott collided with a Ford F-250. I cannot say today I am a Chevy over Ford fan or vice versa since I clearly live cause of Volvo, but a Malibu and an F-250 seems an unlikely match-up, unfortunately. I often still wonder if Scott was wearing that belt buckle that fateful evening for him and his wife. I wonder if he was there with Marcus in spirit as he handed over his belt to wrap as a tourniquet around a stranger's bleeding leg. I often wonder how difficult such an experience had to have been for Marcus, maybe fearing he would have to witness my death and the emotional trauma he had to have been experiencing as he stood by trying to console this screaming woman he had never met.

If you believe in miracles and divine intervention, you cannot possibly see this as anything other than God's hand. Had Marcus and Jesse not been where they were so close, would I have survived? Had Marcus' dad not passed away, would Marcus have been wearing the belt that was wrapped around my leg? How far back in time had God had to go to orchestrate the lives of others to make my near-death experience near and not just death? Like many others have said in their lives, "I would like to ask God that when I get to heaven!" However, I can only imagine it won't even be something that crosses my mind.

I was fortunate enough to not only speak with both of them but also thank them in person for their heroic assistance in one of the most difficult times in my life. They were and are heroes to me.

Borgia

My oldest daughter, Emily, was attending a fairly small catholic high school, Saint Francis Borgia, at the time. She had just completed her junior year with a bright future ahead. I had a lingering bill for that school year. I had put aside just enough to get it paid with my next paycheck, which was to come at the end of June. I was a commissioned employee. Meaning if I didn't work, I didn't get paid. I was paid at the end of the month for the work accomplished the previous month. With everything up in the air due to not being able to work and being bedridden, I was full of worry. I was terrified of how I was going to pay my bills and survive. I was quickly reminded of something so soothing after yet another miracle God performed during my recovery. That was that I was more valuable to God than the birds in the sky, and He provided for them. See, I went up to my daughter's school to pay the bill in faith because I knew it was necessary and again, God in all His glory showed himself in miraculous ways that day.

Because of the small size of my daughter's school, everyone knew of my accident. Upon arrival at her school, I entered the secretary's office which was right in front of Father Mike Boehm's office. As I was telling my story tearfully, he got up from his desk in his office. He walked up to me, and though we might have only spoken a handful of times, he hugged me. He asked me not to write my check just yet and left the office. I sat there waiting for what might have been only a few minutes, but it felt like forever, mostly because of my pain, both physical and emotional. Physical pain was apparent to all, but the emotion was not visible; it was more difficult and intense. It was so fresh that I commonly struggled to speak of my miracle and my incredible blessing and typically sobbed uncontrollably. He returned and informed me that there were enough funds in the reserves that they were able to credit me exactly what I needed to be able to cover my mortgage for the next month that I wouldn't be working. It was an extremely humble moment.

Without a doubt in my eyes, and I pray yours as well, it was just another miracle being performed by my guardian angels throughout my healing process. This is but a mere token of how deep and how far God's love is for you and I. To know in our heart of hearts that even when we don't see it, he's working, and with faith comes blessings beyond measure. This is what I desire for you and I forever and ever AMEN.

Axel

September 11, 2021, my grandson Axel was born. Axel was the son my son Brayden had always wanted. He lived a short life, only 8 months, passing away only 2 days before my car accident anniversary on June 2, 2022. He touched so many of us in a profound way. It was through the loss of Axel that I experienced a great deal of grief beyond one's comprehension. His tiny little life being taken away was a devasting blow to our family. With that loss came the fight for custody of his sister Amara. Had I not been in the car accident only 3 years prior, I would not have had the funds to fight for what I believe was the right thing at the time. In my mind, this is yet another miracle within my story.

The loss of Axel brought out a confidence in me I never thought possible. His death brought so many tears. So much crying and so much heartbreak that I genuinely felt I was never going to stop crying. Then God revealed to me something I didn't see coming, and that was the peace that passes all understanding. I still cry. I still cry a lot, however, the shame that comes with feeling inferior or lacking strength is gone. The emotions that invoke tears in me for whatever reason I have grown to accept, and I believe God can use my pain to help others. Being vulnerable in front of others is just another way that I can reach people for Christ. I am no longer ashamed of my tears, thanks to Axel.

Every day for the first year, I saw a cardinal bird in some way, shape or form. Granted, I live in an area close to Saint Louis. Saint Louis Cardinals baseball is everywhere around here. Sometimes, it was just a cardinal on a stranger's t-shirt in Walmart which seems like a stretch, but I also had a moment where a cardinal bird flew into my bedroom window as I lay in bed crying.

Today, I believe that Axel had a purpose. I believe his life and death are the reason I am stronger than I have ever been in my faith. I learned a valuable lesson in losing him and grieving him. That was my need to rely on God and God alone.

I know today Axel is yet another guardian angel looking down upon us and looking out for us, and we are grateful for the time we had with that little angel.

CHAPTER 3

GRATITUDE

Job

I remember as a young girl when my paternal grandmother Helen would come to visit us wherever we lived. I always enjoyed sleeping with her. She was a Christian woman; she attended church regularly and was an avid Bible reader. I specifically remember her requiring me to read the Bible before bed with her every night as a 5th grader. I was to read the entire book of Job at her requirement if I wanted to sleep with her. Let me just say Job is not child-friendly. There are plenty of happier books in the bible to suggest to a child, but nonetheless, I read it. I was terrified. I'm not 100% sure of her thinking on why she thought it would be best for me to read Job at the age of 11. I can only surmise that she was attempting to put the fear of God in me. That if I knew what God could do to Job then it is wise of me to be on my best behavior, so God doesn't do the same to me.

Job was blameless and upright. He feared the Lord and shunned evil. I was certainly far from that. Satan tried his best and failed with Job. He tried his best and won with me on more than one occasion. For those of you who don't know the story of Job, if you are over 12, I'd highly recommend reading the book. Under 12, expect some potential nightmares. Job had everything his heart desired, and God allowed Satan to take it away to prove how dedicated Job was to Him. His servants, stock, and CHILDREN gone. JOB 10:1: *"I loathe my very life; therefore, I will give free rein to my complaint and speak out in the bitterness of my soul."* Now this I can get my head around. Job was a whinner and a serious complainer. He questioned God so much and didn't understand His thinking.

We are like two peas in a pod on this front. At least inwardly if that makes sense.

After my car accident, on the outside, I was honestly shouting praise that I was alive and grateful for my pain, which meant I was still here. Most of my family would tell you I was tough, strong even, a fighter. That is what I wanted everyone to believe, and it was true. I was happy to be alive, and I wasn't sad and wallowing in my pity on the outside, that is. Oh, but on the inside, I was screaming. I was devasted, confused, and depressed. At the time, I couldn't comprehend or fathom even why I deserved to live. It wasn't the physical pain that hurt me so much; it was the emotional pain of being alive that caused my suffering. What made me so special that He thought I was worthy to still be alive? Truly God reveals it all in His own timing, and being able to sit here today writing these words is proof enough as to why I had to struggle with every little discomfort, whether externally or internally, to be close enough to my Lord and savior Jesus Christ to be sharing this intimate journey with you. The journey of how Jesus opened my eyes to so much of His splendor and greatness through my struggles and sadness. Just like Job.

Addiction

I had never been an addict or even really comprehended an addict's difficulties, though I have had several addicts in my life. I am a decent support person for them, but until this life changer, I had no idea the depths of pain that come with addiction. I was prescribed a very small dose of opiates, a muscle relaxer, nerve pain medication, and an anti-anxiety medication. Knowing how addictive most of the medications were, I was carefully using them to stretch them out if I could. Instead of taking them every 4 hours as prescribed, I took 2 a day. At the time, I thought that it made sense. Yes, I was in more pain, but I knew there was likely little to no chance of getting another prescription for the opiates. You know, the one pill that was helping my pain. Because of the ongoing opiate epidemic, a 40-something grandma certainly isn't likely to get the support that, dare I say, she rightfully deserves. I did get the surgeon to write one more, even smaller prescription. Knowing that was it, I pushed those pills out as long as I could in my system. I knew once I took my last pill, I was going to be in for another hell. I had no idea the mental torture that was creeping in with every hour I pushed myself to go without the medication. I was able to stretch my pain meds, which were enough for 6 weeks for 4 months. Hindsight is always 20/20. I see the error of my ways today. You see, that last pill was the onset of some of the darkest days I have ever been through. I did not think I was addicted because I was using them so sparingly that it didn't even register that by lengthening the medication time in my body, the more dependent I had become on them, curving a bit of physical pain but more importantly, keeping the emotional pain at bay.

HELP!

I remember the first night without the medication like it was yesterday. Ok, let me preface here, I am not a doctor, and I have no medical training other than a WEDMD degree. I know very little of the statistics of things. I could certainly research all the variations to add more fluff and details here, but I am here to give you something more than numbers and hypotheses. All I know is my personal experience, whether from the spectator position or an internal view. So, I digress; the first night without medication was like hell on earth. I had gone over 12 hours without the medication before, so I worried very little about the possible repercussions. I took a muscle relaxer and some melatonin, certain I'd drift off without a problem.

Wow, was I wrong? A night full of fear and phantom pain was in store. I rolled over with a grunt of pain as my cracked sternum still invoked occasional moans to look at my old, trustworthy alarm clock. The time was 1:12 am. My body was drenched in sweat. My organs felt like they were burning on fire in my chest, and my leg had its own heartbeat. I called out to God in agony, and there was a small bit of instant relief. I closed my eyes only to be quickly awakened again at the sound of what I thought was one of my children calling out, "Help!" I flew out of my bed, hobbling towards the door at warp speed as the terrified mothering instinct kicked in, fearing for my babies. I stood at the door listening with intent to determine which way to turn to which child when Michael wheezed out a snore that resembled the "Help" I heard. I turned, giving him the look of death, and returned to bed with a bit of a chuckle. The clock read 1:26 am. Little did I know HELP was going to be something way larger than Michael snoring. I do not remember sleeping that night all that much more. I must have slept some because I dreamed. I heard a lot of sounds that night, cries mostly, some most likely mine but some unknown. Every time my eyes shut, the sound of shattering glass and metal twisting caused them to pop wide open.

My trusted old-school clock from like the 1990's read 1:55 am, 2:37 am, 3:19 am, 4 something, and so on until 7:31 am. I laid there in anguish. I dreamt all night. I felt like I had the weight of the world on my chest that morning. Like every car accident that had ever happened was my fault, and it was my fault that others died, and I didn't. Rationally speaking, this is ludicrous, I know this, but at that very moment, rationality was the furthest thing from my thought process. I hurt so badly that the internal pain was excruciating. I wanted to die to atone for the deaths of everyone else who had ever died in a car accident, and this set the stage for the next several months of survivor's guilt that plagued my every move. Everywhere I went, everyone I saw, I worried. It was debilitating at times internally. All of this was happening so quickly. No one had a clue how overwhelmingly terrifying it was becoming. Even I was not prepared for what was to come next.

It had been less than 48 hours since I was opiate-free, and my traumatic brain injury began to really show itself in ways I wasn't prepared. I was hobbling towards my garage, my cane on my left side; as I opened the door, I heard it again, "Help"! I lost my balance in fear and bounced on my good leg a few steps to catch myself, thankfully. Did I just hear that? This time, it was the middle of the day, and I was alone. I called out, "Hello?" I am not sure who I thought would answer, but that is what I did.

A fear rose in me that was absolutely petrifying. Imagine some unknown distraught voice calling out to you for "Help". Your first thought if, like mine would be, "Ok, where are you so I can help you?" The second thought was that of undeniable, petrifying derangement. It felt almost as if the room were spinning, and my mind was out of control. The disconnection to truth was beyond frightening. I closed the garage door in front of me and sat down in a nearby chair. Put my hands to my temples and called out to God. "Please don't let this happen!" I knew that what I was experiencing was from my traumatic brain injury, but that didn't decrease my fears in any way whatsoever.

Having had education in mental illness, I knew that brain injuries could lead to significant character alterations and many symptoms mimicking schizophrenia. The obvious audible hallucinations were my chief fear at that time, of course. It was just that one word always stinging my soul and invoking a terrifying fear in me every time I heard it.

I reached out to a neurosurgeon for counsel. He, of course, started me on another medication, which I took to no avail. He advised me that after a year, the symptoms of my injuries would become permanent. That was terrifying. I sought out the one true healer to take those four excruciating letters from me. Of course, I can say today that I most definitely should have started with prayer. Again 20/20. "Help" did finally dissipate. I heard it less and less as time went on, but there was never a time that it didn't create an uprising in my blood pressure and the need for God in my life. I cannot encourage you enough when you are feeling that anxiety that the devil thrives on creating in you that you turn to His word and know this; *For God has not given us a spirit of fear, but of power and of love and a sound mind.* (2 Timothy 1:7 NKJ).

Help did finally leave me, that was until God later revealed to me such an amazing gift with "Help," and that was when I reached out to Brian, the tow truck driver, nearly two and half years after our accident, to ask him to meet with me to discuss our accident. When Brian answered the phone with "Hello," it was like he was saying "Help"! Never could anyone possibly understand the immense gratitude and disbelief I experienced with that simple word. The beauty of realizing that "Help" was always a memory from the accident trying to come back during the mental anguish of the first year. This was, without a doubt, the most amazing gift from God. The undeniable clarity of something so special cannot be fathomed. There are no words to express the weight being released off me at that moment. I can only attribute this to God. Had God not put it on my heart to write this for your eyes to see this, I would have never felt the need to make that phone call. That in itself was one of the most revealing miracles I believe God offered me in my journey of following His will for me. You just do not know what God has in store for you when you trust the path He has lined out for you.

Further on, I will share more about my connection with Brian. For now, I need to dive deeper into the battle of emotional pain brought on by the loss of painkillers and the rise of pain.

With every day, I went further and further into a hole. A hole so deep that I couldn't seem to get out of it no matter how hard I tried. With the removal of the painkillers continuing to wreak constant havoc on my mind I was screaming on the inside. It is strange that I write it in that way, using the word mind instead of the body? It was my body that had the need for painkillers, right? Why, then was my soul hurting? It was like an awakening of sorts. Everything seemed harder to see for what it was because my reality had been exponentially altered. Let me explain.

I want any aged person to feel comfortable reading this, but let's assume for a second that you, the reader you are at least in your 30's. Looking back on your youth, specifically between 18-25, give or take, ask yourself, did you feel invincible? Did you throw a little caution into the wind a bit more than you do today? I sure did. I didn't think of what my actions might do to others or myself. The word consequences rarely entered my mind. To clarify, I do not think all humans go through this exactly. I do believe, however, if we really dive deeper into self-discovery about who we were during that time of our lives when we got our first taste of independence, many would assess themselves similarly. It is a moral imperative that I convey this to you with your complete understanding; my new reality was full of consequences. I no longer saw things from the same perspective.

I am reminded of a time I was all wild and crazy about becoming a missionary. I saved, I washed cars, and sold things just to be able to go on my very own missions trip. I didn't go with a group I knew I went with a group of people from an organization called Global Outreach for 14 days to Myanmar. I went in thinking I had no comfort zone. God quickly showed me I did, and I was way out of it. I learned a great deal how to rely on His strength when I was weak. The lack of things that Americans take for granted in Myanmar was overwhelming.

When a father kept trying to get me to take his young daughter with me saying "you mommy" and showing me her gorgeous jet-black hair and piercing eyes of fear, I knew in that moment I was way out of my depth. I will never forget the gratitude I have from seeing those significantly less fortunate people. Perspective, it changed that day. When I went home and fed my young children, and they left half their food on their plates it was like a rainfall of terror raining down on them. I struggled so much with having things, pretty much anything. In time that faded to gratitude to God for what He provided. That one short moment in time when a father was willing to give away his beautiful daughter for what he knew was a better life is one that will always stay with me. If you have a heart for missions or if you want to get outside of your comfort zone for God, try it. You will never regret it. I believe America should require all students to go to a third world country before allowing them to graduate to have a better understanding of how fortunate they really are in this country.

My new reality was one of humility and grace as I trudged through the muck of my emotional instability. The mental anguish I struggled with was hands down the hardest battle I fought against Satan. But let me start with this "I AM VICTORIOUS!" and you can be too.

Depression

I suffered from depression for as long as I can remember. I like to call it seasonal depression. I would start going downhill around mid-November and I'd pick back up sometime right around Valentines. I wouldn't say it was debilitating I muddled through, but I was edgier, short tempered, easily offended and known to cry at the drop of a hat. As I was praying over my pain and asking for guidance and clarity within seconds, I visualized myself slitting my wrist in my big bathtub. Sitting in my big jacuzzi tub filled with water and my bright red blood.

Who would find me like that, my mind wondered? It was a visualization that I did not expect nor could ever imagine the possibility of completing. To be clear I am not suicidal and would never kill myself. I have always thought that to be a cowardly and very selfish act, because all things change and as an adult I can honestly say "this too will pass". The problem wasn't that I wanted to die, the problem was Satan was trying to captivate my thoughts. He was trying to steal God's thunder in my life yet again. I have been active in the mental health community as a volunteer for the National Alliance of Mental Illness since my son at the age of 14 began showing severe signs of mental illness. An illness that has troubled him his whole life. He is hands down one of the strongest individuals I have ever met. The adversity that he is challenged with every day is beyond overwhelming. I'm honored to have in my life not only because God gave him to me. But because of the knowledge and strength I have obtained in educating myself to be a better person for him ultimately helped me draw strength from my relationship with Christ. I believe that because of my knowledge and education in this particular field Satan takes great pleasure in putting me in a place of fear with regards to my mental illness. He is the father of all lies and I am so grateful to be putting a stop to his lies in my life and it is all attributed to my screaming of my eminent death in that deep ravine.

Part of my journey leading up to this realization has to do with my experience as a volunteer educator. For many years I taught a class called Family to Family. It was a free class in which family members of mentally ill people taught other family members of mentally ill people how to be better supporters for their loved ones. With this education I have the knowledge that maybe many don't. That includes many of the symptoms of mental illness such as grandiose thinking and religious obsessions. I began questioning myself, is this a side effect of my depression? Maybe it's my TBI (traumatic brain injury) from my accident. Why am I being drawn to this ideation that I need to tell everyone of my accident and the blessings God bestowed on me. Am I crazy? (crazy isn't a word that we supporters like to use but it seemed very fitting for where I felt God was leading me) I shared my thoughts with Michael and though he wasn't even a believer at the time his response what so perfect I will never forget it. "What if you are?" He spoke. I could only agree that there are a lot of things that are worse to be crazy about. I just wanted to feel like this wasn't going to be some fleeting moment of grace between me and God. I didn't want it to end when my depression (which I no longer claim) wore off in February or when my new norm of brain function had been officially determined. Let it be known that if you are reading this than it was God's will for this to be written, for me to be sharing this story in His name. I truly believe that my mid-life car accident crisis has forever altered the trajectory of my life entirely and I am praising God for it!

My Husband

This new unknown path started with the realization that I didn't even know where to start by sharing my story. God just kept whispering in my ear. "Write the book!" It almost became my life's mantra. Even as I write I still have no clue the magnitude of the future that these words will bring forth in my life. To be honest my faith has become so strong because my God is so powerful and amazing that it doesn't matter if it brings anything to me and mine as long as I follow through on what God has tasked me with, I know where my true rewards will be.

However, my very biggest reward I received from my accident, my diligence in following through, and never giving up on getting these words in print is that of my now husband's salvation. When I realized the extent of what I was being called to do through prayer and petition to God I reached out to my pastor at the time and sought his counsel. The words from his mouth stung like a hot searing poker straight out of the flame.

He informed me in the kindest of ways that in no uncertain terms was I prepared. His words were exactly spoken like this. "Get your house in order!" He recommended I read a little pamphlet size book of only 28 pages *called "My Heart Christ's Home" written* by Robert Boyd Munger. I cannot tell you how many times I have read it to date. He was implying if God wanted to use me there was a lot of things that needed to happen before I even dared to step out for Christ. My home that I needed to get in order was so much wider than I ever could have imagined at the time, but we will start with the biggie! I was living with Michael (not married). That in itself would be a no brainer for me today but at the time though I knew it was a sin I wasn't convicted. On top of that sin, we were unequally yoked because Michael was also an atheist. He was always kind and supportive of my relationship with Jesus. He would attend church with me saying that it was "educational on living a moral life, but he didn't believe in all the Jesus stuff."

Though we had done everything separate from God and of our own free will that was about to seriously change. Soon after my realization of the sin in my life Michael moved out. I began praying, I employed my bible study group to pray for Michael's salvation. After I shared with Michael my need for being equally yoked, we stopped having sex and began dating. This is where our testimonies intertwined.

Based on the subtitle "Husband" I can assume you realize the miraculous outcome. Today we are equally yoked and happily married. That is the power of prayer and without my car accident I do not believe I would be seeing Michael in heaven. Today I can say unequivocally that I would go through it all the physical pain and the emotional pain to know that the man I love will be with me in heaven. There is not enough paper to write on how much gratitude I have for his salvation.

Podcast

Fast forward a few years, still no book. A friend of mine we will call her, Dana shared with me a calling of hers to have a podcast. She felt led after much convincing by God. With years of her praying for "The Thone" our podcast was birthed. Dana's passion is for prayer and the need for everyone to see the powers that come from intercessory and personal prayers. My passion was miracles. Though I knew the book was something I was supposed to be doing I told myself well this is just as good, and God will be satisfied because I am getting my story out there. Remember in the subtitle Help when I said I called Brian to talk about the day we collided, I also wanted to share his and my story on the podcast and that is where Brian and I were fortunate enough to come face to face.

We brought our spouses and met at a Mexican restaurant to discuss our recollection of the accident. You could see the anguish in Brian's eyes as we sat and discussed particular aspects of the incident. I believe the struggles of causing someone else unintended lifelong pain was weighing on both Brian and his wife, Mindy. The gratitude I had at that moment for both of them to be willing to sit with me, how unnatural and uncomfortable that must have been for them both. Walking into a situation with guilty feelings on your back. Fearful of what might come from me in that moment. Honestly not until this very heartbeat did, I realize what a gift from God that really was for me. Neither Brian nor Mindy owed me anything. They didn't have to face me at all. They could have easily blocked my number and never wasted their time with me. But there they were sitting across from Michael and I, their eyes showing their worries about what I was going to say.

There really isn't one thing that didn't amaze me in my journey post-accident and the time with Brian and his wife was no different. My hopes were to give them peace. During dinner

I explained to Brian that I believed he was going to be in an accident that day. An accident that could have easily ended much worse for him. Had I not been there I knew in my heart of hearts that he would not have been sitting across from me at that moment. I visualized the location of our collision for years leading up to our conversation over burritos and there was no way he wasn't going to hit that bridge and go over into the creek had we not collided on that rainy summer evening. Brian like me has a purpose in God's plan and he was not supposed to die that day. I consider myself honored to be the person God used to save him and I held no ill will. After much discussion we parted ways with the intention to later do an episode on my podcast with Dana. Which we did. It was very rewarding and a blessing for us both. I healed more in the three hours I spent with Brian having dinner and doing the podcast than I had healed in the 3 years leading up to our meeting.

The ability to give grace and witness the anguish leave their faces was priceless to me. Rarely do people take the time to connect with those that God puts in our lives through an accident such as mine and Brian's. I believe we could all take a page from Pastor Erik Fitzgerald's playbook.

On October 2, 2006, Erik's wife June and unborn son were killed by Matt Swatzell. Matt was a 20-year-old firefighter who was only a couple miles from home when he fell asleep at the wheel after a 24-hour shift at the firehouse and collided with June's vehicle when he swerved into her lane. Through Erik's devasting loss he had two choices, grace, or vengeance. He chose grace. Not only did Erik forgive Matt, but he also spoke on his behalf in the court proceedings and attended church with Matt. Through the tragic loss Erik and Matt became the strongest of friends. This is just one of the many examples of grace God calls us to have for others.

There were and continue to be so many opportunities throughout my experiencing such a life altering miracle for enormous gratitude. The level of gratitude I have to God most high and the others who were and are still apart, of my life surpassed so much these days that I ever thought possible on June 3rd, 2019.

GOD

CHAPTER 4

No Such Thing as KARMA

Understanding it

Simply put Karma is the understanding by various Middle Eastern religions that your future fate is determined by your past and present existence. With Hinduism being considered one of the oldest religions in history, why then shouldn't that religion be the correct one? Why is Christianity right and Hinduism wrong? There are a couple of reasons I'd like to site for clarity's sake. One being the Christian faith, which worships one God. The only God. I do not pray at an altar before a figure or in some specific direction. Two my go-to for every religion other than Christianity, is that my God is alive. He not only lives within me through the Holy Spirit, but He rose from the dead and is seated at the right hand of our Father. Three and just as powerful as one and two is that just because something is older doesn't make it right. The one true God has been in existence since the conception of time. Christianity is and will always be the world's largest religion because of these three factors and, of course, so much more.

When we take the bible literally (as we should), this concept of free will versus predestination becomes a hot topic for some. If we believe that the theory of Karma is flawed, then we need to answer some questions. In Psalm 139:16, David indicates that God has already recorded every day of my life. How is that possible? He goes on to say that God has laid out every moment of our lives. Where is my free will in that?

I find that a lot of times, when we don't have the infinite knowledge and understanding that God has, we tend to run to a few bible verses on faith and trusting God. Like my go-to, which is when Jesus indicates in the book of Matthew that we need such little faith that it only needs to be the size of a mustard seed to move a mountain. Y'all, just let me say I couldn't even move my full laundry basket this morning, but my faith can move mountains. I am certainly not saying there is anything wrong with going to the bible because, ultimately, the bible is hands down the best source of reference we have. Nearly 600 years since the bible was originally printed for all, it is still on the best sellers list and the most-read book to date. But as my pastor says fact check me. So let's do that.

If we believe Jesus is our savior and that our works are NOT, and I repeat, NOT going to get us to heaven, what does it matter if we are good or evil? If Karma plays no part in his infinite plan for us, why not just accept Jesus into our hearts and go have a great time with the time we have left here on earth. Some little come what may attitude, if you will. If God's got this sucker all mapped out and pre-written, then what?

First off, I believe our free will and our predestination are interwoven together. Just because God has written our life out does not mean that we don't have free will. Let's break it down a wee bit. God allows us to be in control; God allows us to sin, make mistakes, feel pain, experience loss, and bear witness to some pretty heinous stuff in our life span if you really think about it. Conceptualizing that He already knew what sins, what mistakes, what pain, what loss, and what heinous stuff we are to experience seems doable right. I mean He is God. He has the whole plan already laid out, not just yours and my little, tiny part we are playing. The whole kit and caboodle is within His understanding.

The verse that helps me understand the idea of free will and our predestination written out by God controversy is this: *"We may throw the dice, but the Lord determines how they fall." Proverbs 16:33.* Well, there you go, ladies and gentlemen, throwing dice = free will and how they fall = he already knows the end result (predestination).

I have over many years, perfected my slightly overactive imagination. I like to imagine God has this Guinness Book of World Records thick book up there and he's like "Ok gang (His angels of course) we are going to try and get through page one, googolplex and five today (clearly had to research the biggest possible number here). *"Let's make it a great day for as many as we can for my mini me's down there on earth!"* Can you visualize how funny that would be? I can!

A parent who loves their child and wants nothing but what is best for them still should, at some point, let them fail, let them learn from their mistakes, or they will just continue to make the same mistakes which, as we all know, the definition of insanity is doing the same thing over and over and expecting a different result. When we hoover over them and try to save them from every little whoopsie daisy, what have they learned? They learned, plain and simple, I can get away with anything, and Mom and Dad are just going to make the whoopsie daisy go away. What happens when Mom and Dad aren't there anymore? Well, that child, now maybe an adult, has to face a great deal of difficulties and struggles because they weren't given the opportunity to fail and succeed on their own accord. God, in his infinite wisdom, chooses to let us experience pain to teach us so we don't continue to repeat the same mistakes repeatedly in our short time here on earth. Ultimately, God is setting us up for success; we need only <u>be open</u> to learning from our difficult situations as fast as we most possibly can to overcome them.

Jesus Effect vs. Butterfly Effect

Your destiny is determined by the Jesus effect, not the butterfly effect. Our destiny, though God knows how it ends, we do not. If we spend our focus on the wrong effect, we're going to experience the wrong results.

The butterfly effect is about how tiny changes in the grand scheme of things can have complex results. It has a scientific name called sensitive dependence on initial conditions. Like Karma believes what comes around goes around, the butterfly effect believes one butterfly flaps its wings in Brazil, causing a tornado in Texas. The ripple effect of something so small being able to cause something so large and catastrophic is a key component of the chaos theory. If we spend our time focusing on chaos theories in life, we are going to miss out on so many miracles God looks to bless us with.

There are many ways to imagine or portray the Jesus effect because, let's face it, there isn't much that doesn't point back to Jesus. The Jesus effect, in this case, is the idea that if we let him be the effecting source in our lives, than we will experience more of him. We will, by proxy, relate more to him, connect with him, and even crave to be more involved with how He works. You will <u>be open</u> to being used by Him; you will <u>be open</u> to seeing his glorious workings everywhere you turn....even in the tough stuff. I would even challenge you more so during the tough stuff.

Focusing on Jesus in all things and trusting the holy spirit to guide you in the right ways in every aspect of your life is what creates a Jesus-affected destiny. Having the veil lifted from the chaos and seeing Jesus's constant attention to every little detail in your life is liberating. Being liberated from the chaos of the outside world allows us to be more receptive to God's work in our lives and opens our eyes to His intercessions on our behalf.

The cardinal rule

What comes around goes around is the easiest way to verbalize Karma to someone. Did your mother tell you that?

Mine did, darn near every time I even slightly suggested something just the tiniest bit nefarious. Only we were Southern Baptists not Hinduist, and she would say in her most King James version voice she could muster, "Do unto others as you would have them do unto you Trisha." My memory of that started around the age of 6 or 7, and I still hear it today when she catches me being sassy from time to time. I believe the problem with my getting told that more than a few times was because I had a big mouth and would say just about anything that most people would have been wise enough to keep to themselves. Lord knows I am still a work in progress on that one. I do, however, believe today that I should treat people the way I wish to be treated. I love myself enough to try, admittedly though exceptionally hard at times to be kind to others and expect reciprocity that I do not always get. It is a challenge for me to this day to not feel deserving of being treated in a way that is how I perceive that I treat others, not necessarily how they perceive I treat them. Perception is the key to just about everything. If your eyes have been opened to see and your ears have been opened to hear, then how can two people experience the exact things and have two totally different takes on the situation? What I perceive as a miracle, another might call it luck. What I might consider Jesus allowing a loved one to come home to heaven, someone else might say what comes around goes around. Choosing Jesus over Karma, the butterfly effect, or any other worldly direction that Satan tries to sidetrack us on is what makes perceptions vary. The more we make Jesus our focus, the more likely we will be to see things, like just how involved he really is in and how deeply entrenched he is in our lives.

WWJD

There is an intimacy that God craves from you and I that can be a bit overwhelming for me at times. There is a reason we're being advised to put God first, then spouse, then family, and so on. He desires an intimacy so deep in your heart that words don't properly express it; you have to feel it. I am reminded of a movement that took place as I was coming out of my teens in the 90's, and that was WWJD (What would Jesus do). A youth group leader, Janie Tinklenberg, at Calvary Reformed Church in Holland Michigan, encouraged kids to wear friendship bracelets with WWJD. Since friendship bracelets were the rage, they made 300 of them. Never once expecting this movement to become a worldwide phenomenon and continues to be utilized as a tool to encourage everyone to not be sinless and to not be like a carpenter over 2000 years ago but to strive to make choices that are pleasing to God our father. Nearly 30 years later, you can still find over 2000 options of WWJD bracelets on Amazon. Because of its fast-growing popularity, many took the defense and said what Jesus would do isn't necessarily what a young teenager in today's world should do. However, these nay sayers missed the mark and got lost on semantics instead of realizing it was about connecting to Christ in a personal way and creating the intimacy between kids and Jesus. Ask yourself what would Jesus do and then experience how you feel about the answers to achieve the intimacy God desires to have with you. Let Him speak to you every time you ask yourself those four simple words.

To be honest, God doesn't ask for much. He asked for a personal relationship with you. He just wants to be intimate with us and through that intimacy comes insight into His ultimate plan for our lives. The more intimate we try to be with God the more in tune we will be of his working miracles in and around us.

DIG IN

It would be easy if we could get saved and baptized, and a switch would flip in our lives, and we would just suddenly get it. We would not have to work at it. But that is far from what happens in fact many people get saved and feel nothing changed. Sometimes Satan is super ticked; he loses a powerful soul and starts to make their life even more miserable than before in an attempt to make them rethink the whole God thing. It is in those times that I say to you all DIG IN. Soon after I began my work on this book, I realized how little my mind was experiencing negative things. I was happier, more at peace, and it was showing itself quickly to those around me. After several horrific nightmares, and I mean super scary demonic stuff waking me at night I realized Satan couldn't control my thoughts while I was awake, so he infiltrated my sleep where I had little control. It was in that moment I had a choice to let the emotions and negativity that I experienced consume me or choose to DIG IN I obviously dug in or these pages would not be in your hands today.

When I think of digging in, I think of how a batter digs his cleats in the dirt to plant them firmly every time before winding the bat back to prepare for the extremely fast ball being hurled at them. Life is all about the swing, how we handle the hurling balls Satan attempts to either lob at us or something fast ball those painful experiences at us with so much speed we don't even see them coming.

That is why God tells us throughout the Bible, from Genesis (the 1st book in the bible) to Revelation (the last book in the bible) about preparing for a battle. A verse that seems most fitting and that is commonly used is *1 Peter 5:9 "Stand firm against him and be strong in your faith."* Him, of course, being Satan because, in the previous verse, he was prowling around like a lion looking to devour us. No matter how we look at it whether we dig in, stand firm or get ready for the swing, we must be prepared for the sometimes-excruciating things that Satan will attempt to throw at us in our lives. I'd like to give you this bit of encouragement Satan doesn't attack those he isn't worried about. That isn't to say that those who are atheists or non-believers won't have difficult times they will. It just means because we live in a world full of sin it is unavoidable and being prepared for it and knowing how to receive it when it comes will in part give you peace as well as even joy if you let it.

James, Jesus's own brother who was martyred for his belief and teachings wrote very first in the book of James 1:2-4 of the importance of being prepared and how to handle opposition. *"Dear brothers and sisters, when trouble of any kind comes your way, consider it an opportunity for great joy. For that when you know your faith is tested, your endurance has a chance to grow. So let it grow, for when your endurance is fully developed you will be perfect and complete needing nothing."* To clarify James meant perfect in your faith no one other than Jesus is, was or will be perfect no matter how hard we try. However, getting on board with joy during troubles is one of the many ways God instructs us on how to open ourselves freely to Him. Ultimately once we switch our mindset, we start seeing all of God's involvement and the dot to dots take hold a picture and we see everything so much clearer.

The last two words of those verses really says it all you could close up shop, call it a day, end on a high note whatever you want to call it with those last two words alone. "Needing nothing!" I like the message version of the bible it states it as *not deficient in any way.*

Needing nothing or not being deficient can be described as contentment. It is a sense of peace or happiness that invokes a feeling of fulfillment. Imagine your worst fear, whatever it is in your life right now. Give it just a second of your time and I say a second because we don't want to give it a foothold, but I do want you to consider it being completely eradicated from your life. You might be thinking, "Impossible". I say to you all things are possible with God being our number one focus. Even the trenches we get ourselves in. Even the troubles James spoke of in chapter one, and dude, did James get himself into some trouble for his beliefs.

Scholars differ on whether James is truly the half-brother of Jesus or just another James with a dad named Joseph and a brother named Jesus, and as much as I enjoy history, I have to say either way, who really cares. James the Just was an important figure in the early decades of establishing Christianity. The book of James can easily be considered a how-to book on Christian living. His teachings in his five-chapter book should be a true testimony to how God works in our lives. Think about it; let's just say for argument's sake, James was Jesus's brother. Can you imagine how difficult of a role he played in following Jesus's teaching and leading and establishing the Christian church under persecution? The difficulties that would come with not only being called to follow God's prompting in his life just like you and I are called but to do it as the messiah's brother. Yikes, that is a level of distinction that I think would be a bit frightening. Have you ever had to follow in someone's footsteps, a sibling, a coworker or other? Imagine those footsteps were perfect. Again, I say yikes! James was even martyred for his faith in Jesus in a gruesome way. People are still to this day persecuted for their beliefs maybe not thrown off cliffs and stoned to death, but persecution comes in many forms. James how to book definitely teaches us the value of finding contentment in our walk with Jesus. How to accept the good with the ugly and stay on task for Christ.

Faith over Fear

Satan takes great pleasure in taking hold of our fears and running with them. Worrying is a big one in most of our lives. Whether we want to admit it or not, we all worry about something. There are several kinds of worry. Some are small or big personal worries like will I get to work on time or death in your family. Other types of worry are outside of our immediate grasp, not so personal but still just as cumbersome. For instance, the government, the starvation of children around the world etc. I am reminded of my granddaughter at the age of 3 dancing in front of the television to *"Let It Go"* from the Disney movie *Frozen*. Or the many times I have dropped off a suitcase of concerns at the father's feet only to pick it up again and again with the mindset that I can do it better because of my impatience or because I'd like to say I don't want to burden the Lord with my problems. Ha, what a joke. It is all about not relinquishing control to God. Let me tell you something the more you allow worry to be your problem and not allow God to take the wheel like Carrie Underwood sings you are giving Satan the "W". Honestly, I am pretty competitive and when I look at it as giving Satan the win I get a bit heated. I do not like to lose do you? I mean who really does? Let go and let God, and the battle is won in your heart and in your mind against the devil's trickery.

A one-and-done would be great, right? In order for unity with Jesus, because we live in a world that is constantly trying to beat us, we have to make a daily commitment to trust Him. For us to really bear witness to His miracles in and around our lives we need to accept that this too will pass and that yours and my problems and troubles are not even remotely too big for God.

Faith over fear is a commonly used statement these days; you know the cute little signs you find in all the gift boutiques and antique malls. Though it is a catchy phrase there is a lot packed into it in those three little words. It is literally a statement that could be defined as God versus Satan or good versus evil. Faith is complete trust and confidence in something. Faith in God is not only confidence it is a belief that God has got our back. Not only in easy stuff, not only in the bad stuff but in **all** things. Faith is accepting that God knows what we need and what we don't need and accepting His will over ours. It is typically evident in someone who is faithful to God's will in their life. The commonly used phrase that I hear is they have God's favor. This is because their faith produces fruit, and that fruit makes God happy, which in turn gives Him the desire to favor them. Well, I want that, don't you? I want to know that if I lose that job, a better one is on the horizon. I want to know that if I lose that family member that God has a purpose for my pain and a reason for my struggles, and a reward for my faithfulness. If I stay faithful to His promises, it is a 100% guarantee that I will bear witness to His purpose. I need only BE OPEN to seeing and accepting His will. C.S. Lewis a well-known author best known for his Chronicles of Narnia series said it well when he said, *"To have Faith in Christ means, of course, trying to do all that He says. There would be no sense in saying you trusted a person if you would not take his advice."*

Fight the Crack Attack

Fear, on the flip side, is the opposite of faith, and it leads us down a path of destruction. It can take us away from God and lead us into darkness. Satan is the master of deception. He takes great pleasure in finding our cracks. The cracks that may not seem that deep or that wide can quickly become all-consuming crevasses and overwhelm us. We've all experienced this in one way or another. For example, have you ever had a fearful thought, and you captivated that sucker and thought to yourself, "Yay me thank you, Jesus" only to have it rears its ugly head again? Sometimes again and again? This happens to me all the time, and when I realize it, I find that the more I take it to God in prayer and the more I find his answers in the Word, the smaller the cracks begin to become. The more I am freed from the grasp the devil tries to have on me and my life. Fear keeps us from having this impenetrable shell to ward off the inevitable crack attacks. Ultimately the less fear more faith mentality is one of the many ways that God instructs and guides us to bearing witness to his miracles in and around our lives.

I am reminded of the Japanese pottery art called kintsugi. The idea of breaking a bowl into several pieces and then putting the pieces back together and then filling the cracks with gold. God is our gold; our lives are the bowl. The bowl holds our soul, our emotions, our character, and most importantly our heart. If we allow God into the very cracks of our lives, the devil's attempt at our cracks will be futile. Don't fall victim to the crack attacks be filled with God's gold.

Part of living the unavoidable sinful lives we live is accepting the consequences of our actions. Many times, we don't even realize the connections. I sinned last week; I didn't repent, and now this is happening. It isn't something many of us conceptualize very often, especially in our daily lives. Being open to this concept is like asking a toddler to accept that their parents know what is best for them even when they are being punished for their wrongdoings, it is unnatural. Imagine if you will a 5-year-old saying, "Yes, please, I deserve that spanking for playing in the fireplace." Or "Can I please go to bed early because I refused to listen in the grocery store." Are you laughing yet? I sure am. That doesn't happen even the non-strong-willed child would not be so accepting. Let me tell you that sure would-be nice though right! As we mature in Christ and become more and more like Him it stands to reason that we must accept the bad with the good. I am not saying that all things that happen in your life are due to your lack of repentance or the sin in your life. I am saying those certainly play a factor and the more we repent for our obvious sins the closer we become to God. The closer we are the more understanding we have of His inner workings and desires for our happiness. Like any good father, He only wants the best for you and me, but He isn't going to let us get away without consequences for our actions.

When I think of Paul telling the Romans in Romans 7:15-17, I am filled with *hope "I don't really understand myself, for I want to do what is right, but I don't do it. Instead, I do what I hate. But if I know that what I am doing is wrong, this shows that I agree that the law is good. So, I am not the one doing wrong, it is sin living in me that does it."* These verses should give you an immense sense of hope. These words are from the man whom God used to write nearly half of the New Testament. Four of those books were written letters from a prison cell. Paul's incarceration, whether right nor wrong, was a consequence for his actions and look at how God used that time in prison. Nearly two millennials later those letters are still being read today. Now I ask you, with that realization, how do you define that? Do you see it as Karma, pure luck, or God's infinite plan at work in Paul's mess?." If God can use Paul's messes in such a profound way, he can certainly use ours. And if Paul, the writer of half of the New Testament, someone with a great deal of clout back in the day, can admit that he does what he hates because of sin, then we should be able to accept our sins and the consequences that come with those sins. Once we accept our sins and recognize them for what they are we are then at a crossroads. Do we take the road less traveled?

My father was a lover of poetry. He would write poems for my mother regularly, and he would read books of poetry aloud to me often. Robert Frost was one of his favorites. Frost's poem *"The Road Not Taken"* is one of the most utilized American written poems. It has been used in everything from commencement speeches to television commercials.

> Two roads diverged in a yellow wood,
> And sorry I could not travel to both
> And be one traveler, long I stood
> And looked down one as far as I could
> To where it bent in the undergrowth;

> Then took the other, as just as fair,
> And having perhaps the better claim,
> Because it was grassy and wanted wear;
> Though as for that the passing there
> Had worn them really about the same,
>
> And both that morning equally lay
> In leaves no step had trodden black.
> Oh, I kept the first for another day!
> Yet knowing how way leads on to way,
> I doubted if I should ever come back.
>
> I shall be telling this with a sigh
> Somewhere ages and ages hence:
> Two roads diverged in a wood, and I—
> I took the one less traveled by,
> And that has made all the difference.

Frost is referencing his choices in life and the feelings about those choices. God invites us to take the road less traveled by. Frost implied that making that decision to take the less traveled path is what made all the difference, even when he couldn't see the future through the woods. Walking the grassier way that needs wear is what brings about a deeper connection to God.

Choosing to live a morally correct life continues to increase our favor and our connection to Christ. When faced with the option of good versus evil, I believe most would say I choose good. Well, what if it is offered in a shiny package or everything you thought you ever wanted? It may look good. I mean, it might look like there is nothing better. Do you seek God first? I was recently faced with a situation that seemed just too good to be true. Something so perfect you'd say it made all the sense in the world to go for it. Knowing that the devil is always working to corrupt our walk with Jesus and create a disconnect from God, I took it to God in prayer. A simple one-liner *"If it's your will Lord open the doors if it isn't your will shut them quickly and give me peace."* Folks, it was a for sale sign in a front yard and I couldn't even get in the door to see the property. As painful as the loss of something we think is so perfect can be I had great peace because I knew God wasn't necessarily say "No Trisha." He was saying "Not now, I have something bigger and better for you planned just you wait and see." Truthfully at that moment it stunk. I was bummed and disappointed but accepting His word as truth gave me peace because that is what I asked for. Jesus said it point blank in John 14:27 *"I am leaving you with a gift - peace of mind and heart, And the peace I give is a gift the world cannot give. So don't be troubled or afraid."*

Since the beginning of creation, everything in life turns back to Jesus. He is the reality of everything positive, being God's answer to everything we deal with. Jesus being the son of God and the part of the Holy Trinity that took on human flesh He has the direct connection to our past and our future. He is and will always be the only sinless being in existence. When the light flickers on over our heads and the idea of God's ownership over everything becomes apparent, we start to realize that our best course of action should be pleasing the owner of all things. Let's be the teacher's pet.

Looking back on my childhood growing up, I made some poor decisions, okay a lot of poor decisions. I would say I was probably never a teacher's pet. I was a stubborn, strong-willed child who didn't listen to those who were wiser and knew better. When teachers look back on their careers, there is very likely any remembering me fondly. I had to learn most things the hard way and that included pushing the limits at every opportunity. I got into trouble (mostly for talking) too much. I was most likely a bit of an embarrassment to my parents, and I felt like I knew what was best for me. Can a get an amen at least in solidarity? Today I can say each and every one of those choices molded me like the potters clay that I am, into exactly what God intended for me and my life. Hard roads and difficult choices can lead us to not only salvation but to a better appreciation for everything God has blessed us with. The harder the life's choices the more likely we are to be able to look back over our lives and say God was with me even when I didn't realize it. I am blessed to be here, and everything, absolutely everything is because of Jesus not Karma.

CHAPTER 5

Miracles

Greatest Miracle Ever

I don't want to come across uber preachy because I am not a preacher, at least not today. However, miracles are kind of my thing. Ever since God saved me, I look for them everywhere. It is my passion. I enjoy seeing God working in my life and the lives of others. I devour stories past and present that support God's presence in our lives. So, buckle up, buttercup; you are in for a ride in this chapter.

The very first sentence in the bible is, and will always be, no matter how long of an existence there is, the greatest miracle ever, and that is Genesis 1:1: *"In the beginning God created the heavens and the earth."* Trust me, I tried to find one bigger to start this chapter off with, and it just isn't possible. When you take a second and think about the magnitude of what that looks like it is beyond comprehension. God was already here because He is the Alpha, meaning the beginning. He has always been and always will be. Close your eyes right now and look at the back of your eyelids. That is what I do when I want to imagine before God created the heavens and earth. Darkness, just complete nothingness. And then, poof, heavens and earth are created. But there was still darkness, and in Genesis 1:2 God said, *"Let there be light"*.

I imagine opening my eyes to the brilliance of the brightest light possible, like staring directly at the sun just seconds after waking up, and your eyes haven't quite focused. I am reminded of fifth grade when my entire class was shuffled outdoors and told not to look up at the sun but to look in a shoebox created for us to see the results of a solar eclipse. I looked. It hurt, and

I wear glasses today; who knows if it was from that or not. But I do know I saw rings around everything for the rest of the day.

Scientists who disagree with the concept of creation are more prone to believe that it is the chicken or the egg theory that came first. Ok, the Big Bang theory, but seriously, I like my name for it better. Meaning that there was nothing, and then somehow out of nowhere this star appears and over billions of years there is the big bang, everything exploded, and then evolves into what we see today. Two questions immediately come to my mind. One, what made the star that banged? Two, and this is the one that seems more sensible to me: how did an explosion create something that is so orderly and appears to be by design? A brilliant scientist with what is believed to be one of the highest IQ scorers ever, Sir Isaac Newton, is quoted as saying, *"Atheism is so senseless. When I look at the solar system, I see the earth at the right distance from the sun to receive the proper amounts of heat and light. This did not happen by chance."* Because Newton's' theory was based on the concept that the solar system was directed by the hand of God, his overall theory was discredited with an explanation of how things move within our solar system years after his death.

Whether his theories are accurate or not remains to be seen until the time of which we see the back of our eyelids for the last time. I do, however, appreciate his intellect and the credentials that established him as a genius of historical proportions. There is something to be said about someone so deeply entrenched in intellectual science who chooses to lean to theology for the unknown. Creation is and will always be one of the many unanswered questions we, as believers know that we know the answer, and non-believing scientists will attempt to find answers.

Defining Miracles

The enlightenment that I hope you gain as you read on will not only give you all a perspective of how God works His daily interventions in our lives, but my hope is that it will truly expand your comprehension of how deep, far, and wide God's love for you really is. I pray that these words permeate your soul and bring you to a place of deep connection to Christ and His unimaginable passion for us all.

Wayne Grudem a Harvard educated professor of theology, states in his book *Systemic Theology*, *"A miracle is a less common kind of God activity in which he arouses people's awe and wonder and bears witness to himself."* I struggled a great deal with these words, so much so that I considered not including them. Grudem is certainly well educated, and I have no reason to doubt his intellect, but the idea that miracles are "Less common" seems limiting, and I do not desire to limit God. To be fair, I do believe Grudem was more specifically indicating miracles being performed in the moment, like laying hands on someone who is lame, and they get up and walk. Yes, I can get on board with the concept that those with the spiritual gift of performing miracles through the Holy Spirit on the spot are not necessarily gifted with a daily dose of big miracle performances.

Grudem goes on to say that "other definitions fall short; miracles are not simply God's intervention in the world (as if He does not intervene every second), nor are they exceptions to natural law (as if the laws of nature function apart from God's providential hand), nor are they simply events that natural causes cannot explain (as of God does not use natural causes in working miracles.)".... "Some answers to prayer may fit this definition, while others may not, but for both, we can give thanks to God."

I am in awe by God. I am in awe by His daily interventions in my life and the life of those around me. Whether it was by prayer and petition or if it is simply my awareness of God's working in my life. Whether Grudem's definition is correct or not is not the true point being made. The concept of God's love is. The fact that He loves us so very much that He has given us free will to do as we wish but is also behind the scenes loving and supporting us by showing us compassion through intervening on our behalf when we need Him most.

Miracles are meant to be confirmation of God's work. Confirmation that He is available to us today, not just as He was in the Bible. Miracles can inspire those who don't believe and lead them on a path to a personal relationship with Jesus. Hebrews 2:4 aligns me with this thinking *"And God confirmed the message by giving signs and wonders and various miracles and gifts of the Holy Spirit whenever He chose."* God's message is not obscure nor dependent on blind faith. It is easy to say I accept this but not that when it comes to God's word. Yes, there are many interpretations of the Word, different versions, and different opinions, but it is necessary to follow every word and every interpretation that God puts on your heart because, ultimately, this is your walk with Christ. This is your interpretation of God and your personal relationship with Him. So be open to His intervention and look for His interactions, however big or small, as a way of supporting and confirming your connection to God.

Types of Miracles

There are 4 types of miracles. They are healing miracles, exorcisms, natural miracles, and restoration miracles. It's important for us to understand these 4 types and their roles within our lives, and how they can strengthen our connection to God.

Healing Miracles

A healing miracle is defined as to make whole again. To right a physical wrong in one's life, to make free from injury or disease. The Bible is riddled with healing miracles. One of my personal favorites is, after all, the name of this book and the concept of being open to God's miracles in our lives. Mark 7:32-35 reads, *"A deaf man with a speech impediment was brought to him, and the people begged Jesus to lay his hands on the man to heal him. Jesus led him away from the crowd so they could be alone. He put his fingers into the man's ears. Then, spitting on His own fingers, He touched the man's tongue. Looking up to heaven, He sighed and said, "Ephphatha," which means, "Be opened!" Instantly the man could hear perfectly, and his tongue was freed so he could speak plainly!"* Do you ever read over something or skim over it and not really let the words sink into your soul? I do all the time. But this particular story was one of immense depth and relevance to me and my life. God is so good with repetition, and it took multiple attempts for me to really get it and be open to God's work in my life through this passage. Further in this chapter, you will read stories of healing miracles that are continuing to happen every day.

Exorcism Miracles

An exorcism miracle is considered expelling or removing an unwanted spirit from a person or a place. Demonic possession was real then, and it is real today. When I think of exorcisms, I can't help but think of the 1973 movie *The Exorcist* and Linda Blair's head-spinning projectile vomiting. I can understand how that iconic horror film that is now 50 years old still lends itself to extreme exorcism thoughts for believers and nonbelievers alike. Jesus performed difficult and easier exorcisms. Mark 5:2-13 is a well-utilized example of how Jesus removed a demon from a horribly afflicted man into approximately 2000 pigs, and the possession of the pigs led them down an embankment into a lake to drown. Another Jesus just informs a mother his daughter was healed in Mark 7:24-30. It shares of a lesser-known exorcism that Jesus performed because of a gentile mother's faith. He did not even need to lay eyes on her daughter to remove the demon. Demonic spirits are running rampant in the spirit world, and though it is not something Christians like to admit, we too can be afflicted with demonic spirits whether we have the light of the Holy Spirit living in us or not. We need to be aware of the devils constantly prowling around like a lion looking to devour us (1 Peter 5:8). Deliverance from demonic spirits that are plaguing Christians is happening every day as well and will be shared like the healing miracles further in this chapter.

Nature Miracles

Nature miracles are events that defy the natural order of things within nature. I love pithy quotes, and one that I find true to my heart is from the author of *"Every Day Spirit,"* Mary Davis *"To walk into nature is to witness a thousand miracles."* If I am awed by God in things of nature, does that make it miraculous? I don't know how the awe of a sunrise on a crisp fall morning doesn't get your heart pumping. Or the amazing Seqouia trees towering over 350 feet in California can take your breath away. I have come close to nearly wrecking my car to try to get a better view of an orange harvest full moon. We need only be open to seeing all of the glorious living creatures as God's natural miracles in our lives. Jesus's very first miracle he performed was considered a natural miracle. In John 2:1-11 Jesus and His disciples attended a wedding in which the supply of wine ran out on the third day, which was only halfway into the typical 5-7 day wedding festivities. For those of you who don't know the story, this miracle stunned the master of the ceremony when he stated to the bridegroom, *"A host always serves the best wine first. Then when everyone has had a lot to drink, he brings out the less expensive wine. But you have kept the best until now."* The most important aspect to consider is the unnatural nature-altering miracle that, of course, became the catalyst for Jesus' miracle He performed from that day forward.

Restoration Miracles

Restoration is described as bringing something back to its original state. This type of miracle is considered to raise the dead and restore life. Modern-day medicines and tools have made restoration miracles happen all the time. There are many stories today of restoration and after-death experiences that can be attributed to restoration miracles. Truly, what a testimony to God's presence in our lives when one has died and been brought back to life. Putting aside the idea that a human being could have anything to do with truly restoring life is how we are called to be open in today's culture to restoration miracles. I'd like to suggest that those who have experienced a restoration miracle today they are no longer in their original state but that they experienced a transformation miracle. Transformed by God through the restoration of their lives. How powerful would that testimony be?

Jesus performed several restoration miracles. The one that gets me every time is the full story of his restoring Lazarus his dear friend in John 11:1-44. Short and sweet version is Jesus knew His friend was going to die, and He waited, and on the fourth day of his death, He restored him. I get caught up in John 11:39 when Martha says, *"Lord, he has been dead for four days. The smell will be terrible."* I have to admit I watch a lot of crime shows so that is where my knowledge comes from on this topic. But, considering there was no embalming and though the scholars believe that Jesus raised Lazarus in later winter, early spring, it would still be pretty stinky. There are five stages of decomposition, and based on the timeline, Lazarus would have already been actively in stage one, which is known as the fresh stage/self-digestion stage.

In this stage, rigor mortis would have set in, creating a stiffness due to lack of blood flow, and the internal cells would have begun literally eating away at themselves from the inside out. Lazarus's body would have most likely also experienced stage two, which is called bloating. Bloat is a build-up of gases brought on by bacteria. Many of the gases produce maggots, which begin to feed on dead tissue. This stage also includes livor mortis, which is blood pooling in certain parts of the body. AND.... Jesus shouts, "Lazarus, come out!" and Lazarus appears covered in grave clothes. Jesus is then quoted as saying, "Unwrap him and let him go!" John 11:43-44. I often wonder how Lazarus looked and the healing within his body that God performed through Jesus on that day. How unbelievable that site must have been for Lazarus's family, the apostles, and the onlookers. Watching as the stiff, bloated maggot-covered man walked from out of a tomb. It was but a prelude to come of what restoration miracle God would preform next, that being Jesus's resurrection. I encourage you to take the time to read the story in its entirety, as it really speaks to Jesus' pain about following God's will and His emotions on that day.

Interpreting Miracles

Miracles were the same then as they are now; they have not changed because God has not changed. It is the interpreters that have changed. When we read these amazing stories within the Bible of Old Testament miracles of God seemingly taking the Israelites through one miraculous event to the next. Then we read in the New Testament Jesus's proof of His anointing as the son of God through His miracles. The biggest being His resurrection, of course. After Jesus returned to be with the Lord, the Holy Spirit began working through apostles and performing just as similar miracles. It begs the question of why are we, as modern-day Christians, not experiencing these colossal miracles. We are not interpreting them as miracles. We are not seeking them out and experiencing them for ourselves because we have been conditioned and closed off from the idea that God still desires to show you His very presence in your life.

It boils down to making the commitment to saturate yourself with God. Ask yourself how much time do you spend in the world versus how much time you spend with God? Do you worry about where your next meal is coming from so much that you spend all your efforts working to make ends meet? Doesn't God make it pretty clear in Matthew 6:31-34 *"So don't worry about these things, saying, 'What will we eat? What will we drink? What will we wear?' These things dominate the thoughts of unbelievers, but your heavenly Father already knows all your needs. Seek the Kingdom of God above all else, and live righteously, and He will give you everything you need."* That is not to say don't work; it's sincerely meant to encourage you that we are supposed to be working for Christ and in Him. I am in no way encouraging you to be unemployed, only to do everything as if you are doing it for the Lord. Let God sink in. Allow Him into every aspect of your life. Let Him permeate your being. God already knows everything going on in your life and those around you. He knows the grand plan, and He is calling you to fully surrender yourself and to let Him be more in you than you are in the world.

Those who believe miracles aren't happening today are the ones who aren't looking for miracles, and once you've opened your heart fully to God's infinite plan and allowed Him into every facet of your life, you will begin to see the splendor of His work. And seeing is believing.

Praying For Miracles

I wish I could say every time I prayed for a miracle, God answered it just as I had hoped. Wouldn't that be absolutely wonderful if every time we felt like what we wanted at that very moment God gave us? Guess what? That isn't going to happen. A woman I once called my spiritual mother who has since gone on to be with God told me once, "God answers all prayers in 3 ways. Yes, No, and Not now." I was a baby Christian at the time, and I remember thinking I would try that with my children as a tactic, and "Not now" was like the kiss of death to my kids. "Not now" for me was like a torturous case of tinnitus (ringing in the ears) as it led my children to ask over and over again with incessant vigor. I think about God responding, "Not Now," and my behavior being just like my children just hounding God till I get what I would say is a better answer than "Not Now!" I can easily attribute that to my lack of patience, which God is always teaching me the importance of that one. But even the most patient person can honestly say how dissatisfying "Not Now" can be.

They are just two words in the dictionary that shouldn't be put together if you ask me. The more I analyzed the "Not Now" theory of God's communication, the more it leans itself too much to No, I think and that is why I was turned off by that analogy. But even more so than its leaning direction was the concern that it implies maybe God doesn't know what He is doing and He's figuring things out. As we well know, God knows the plans He has for us. He's already seen the last page of the playbook; you can be sure of that. So, I started to see my prayers being answered differently. I saw the Yes prayers being answered, and I was joyful.

I saw the No Prayers being rejected, and I was humbled under the conviction that my God has something better for me even when it hurt. Even when I was in the darkest of dark holes in my life. I realized, though, that the miracle I prayed for wasn't answered in the way I expected. God had something better. And then, I took it to the next level with the realization that "the better" I can expect might not be for me but for someone else who needed it more. You see, that is accepting that God has this infinite plan far from us to even begin to comprehend. Accepting my cross, picking it up, and being grateful for the yeses we do receive because in the doom and gloom I am throwing at you right now, it's important to point out, we don't deserve any yeses. But by the grace and mercy God gave us through sacrificing His sinless son, we are forgiven and made new in him.

Now, on the brighter side, God looks at us as His children. You can feel that love even if you don't have kids, even if you have bad parents. You know what that love is or should feel like. God is and will always be the only one who really truly knows all of us from the inside out, no stone unturned in our lives. Every dark little, messy, displeasing thing you and I have ever done. He knows it all and wants to have an intimate relationship with us despite it all. That is the kind of love God offers. So, when you and I are despondent at life's painful experiences, we can take comfort in knowing that there is only one who can offer us that agape love because there is only one who truly knows us and wants nothing but the best for us always.

Stories of Miracles

The last section was a bit negative, and I've spent too many years in therapy to leave things like that, so I need to include that praying for miracles is important. It brings about a sense of realization that God is listening to our requests. Here are some absolutely amazing stories of miracles that will prove that Yes is the answer God wants to give us like any Abba would.

It was a warmer than usual Martin Luther King Day in 2015 in Lake Saint Louis when John Smith plunged into a lake he and his friends had stood on just the evening before. After over 15 minutes in the water and a presumed 40-plus minutes of not breathing, his mother stood over him, touching his lifeless, cold gray foot. She began to pray, pray loudly. Joyce said, "The minute I prayed, 'Holy Spirit, please come and give me back my son!' his heartbeat started." The prognosis was still grim; with a body temperature of 88 degrees, the doctors had little hope. None had seen anyone survive with this level of blood PH levels this low. He was rushed to Children's Hospital, and confirmation was made quickly that John had multiple organ failures. His mother got angry because why would God give him back only to take him away again. The doctor "Told me that John wasn't going to live through the night and if he lived, he was going to be a vegetable," Joyce told *People magazine*. "And he made me mad. Because God had already assured me this was going to be okay." Five pastors began praying with Joyce and her family, and at the astonishment of the doctors but not to Joyce, her son John walked out of the hospital with complete brain function in just 3 weeks' time. One of John's doctors, Dr Jeremy Garrett, declared to KSDK, "It was a bonafide miracle!" Joyce wrote a book about their experience called The Impossible in 2017, and a movie was made of their story in 2019 called Breakthrough. It is a miraculous read and a great film, two thumbs up!

I cannot think of a better example of a restoration miracle in today's society than that of a mother's prayer for her son's life to be answered. God is still working people! Today! In our time in our lives, we need only to be open to see it.

An example of a healing miracle that has recently taken place in my life is that of my now 80-year-old mother's life. She was diagnosed with a large tumor in her breast in 2001. She went through chemotherapy to shrink the tumor and had a lumpectomy. 2002, the tumor remerged, and she had a mastectomy. With the reoccurrence, the prognosis was likely to be another reoccurrence. Fast forward to 2023, and my mother had continually gotten positive mammograms with no signs of reoccurrence. That is itself a miracle, in my opinion. She went to the doctor for a spot on her tongue, which turned out to be cancer. We were all worried, of course, however, this cancer was not the same kind, nor was it invasive, and she had it removed with positive results.

Due to the fact she had previously had cancer in her body, the doctors decided to do a full body PETSCAN. The PET showed a large tumor in her same breast tissue with it in the lymph nodes. The PET also lit up on her right hip, indicating the likelihood that the cancer had metastasized to her bones. The first part of the miracle was tongue cancer. Had she not had the non-invasive cancer on her tongue, there would have been no PETSCAN. Since she had recently had a mammogram, there would not have been another for a year, giving the cancer even more time to grow.

My mother is one tough cookie and one that I am honored to know. Her faith has always been an example of power in the midst of my struggles as I strive to continue my walk with Christ. This situation was no different. She had the lymph nodes removed and began healthy choices, not conventional medicine, which drove me crazy. I just wanted my mom to be well. She started eating a large number of apricot seeds and Ivermectin. She had hands laid on her by a dear friend, and she assured her that she was healed. Now, here I am, someone who loves miracles and takes great pleasure in learning of miracles, but when my mom said, "I am healed," outwardly, I was supportive, but on the inside, God knew I was battling her decisions. Her faith was unshaken, and her last PETSCAN showed zero, that's right, zero signs of cancer anywhere in her body. Her doctor was in awe. Though I shouldn't have been, I was awed by the miracle God bestowed on my mother through the power of prayer. She has been blessed with many healing miracles through her life, and I have been blessed to bare witness.

Exorcisms are a scary way of looking at God's miracles; I don't know, is it just me? I mean, I keep going back to the priest, and head spinning. However, deliverance from demonic spirits is taking place today in our midst. For Christians to believe that they are not afflicted by these demons is a miss. Demonic spirits come in many forms. From the spirit of greed, spirit of lying, spirit of gossip, spirit of anger, spirit of lust, spirit of pride, spirit of gluttony, spirit of sexual immorality spirit of fear and worry and the list could go on and on. Everything that is a sin has a spirit attached to it. Anything that is not of God (i.e. good) then Satan (i.e. bad) has his hands in it. We are not immune to having these spirits attach themselves to us and take control of our lives. We'd all like to think being the salt and light of the earth, as Jesus claimed we are in Matthew 5: 13-14, gives us some kind of hedge of protection from these spirits, and it just doesn't. In fact, I would say it makes us more vulnerable. Satan desires to steal our thunder. The more we do for God, the more Satan despises us. The more he despises us, the more he sends his demonic minions to infiltrate our thoughts and our actions. Roughly a third of Jesus's ministry surrounded deliverance. He desires to deliver us from unclean spirits that plague us, and though I do not believe my head will be spinning, I know that the more I draw nearer to God, the more the demonic spirits try to infiltrate my life. The more I write this book, the more I struggle with the spirit of pride. Pride is Lucifer's sin. Thinking he was better than God was the ultimate proverbial slap in the face to God. Here I am thinking because I am feeling so close to God in this moment that so and so just isn't getting it right like I am. Like all of a sudden, I am some all-knowing, and others are not. I bind that spirit daily because I do not want to judge anyone.

Seventeen-year-old youth pastor Vlad Savchuk's first experience in demonic possession was one night after a church service; an Italian gentleman received Jesus as his savior, and as the congregation trickled out of their seats, leaving the church fairly empty, the gentleman began to tell his story. He shard his involvement in witchcraft and Satan worshiping. Vlad knew from his upbringing that this man was going to need to repent and renounce those spirits, and he asked if the man would repeat a prayer with him. As they were repeating the prayer together, Vlad was encouraged by the holy spirit to not touch the man as many people do in prayer but to back away from him. As the gentleman continued to speak, his face churned, and his body began to contort. His words became jumbled, and he could not pronounce the name of Jesus. His appearance gave off the vibe that he wanted to punch those there.

When the man was finally able to say the name Jesus Vlad commanded the demon to leave the man. The man screamed out and collapsed. At that point, the man appeared dead. Vlad believed at that moment after checking his pulse, "We killed a guy." Vlad was reminded of Mark 9:14-29 where a boy was possessed and appeared dead, and Jesus picked him up, and he stood. So, Vlad helped the man to his feet. The gentleman told the story of hearing a voice telling him to punch them. He said I am so glad you held me back, or I would have hurt you. Vlad nor anyone held him back as they had all stepped away. Vlad will tell you today he believes the angels of God held him back and kept the man from the demon punching anyone. Demonic possession is real and should not be discounted as it seems to be in so many churches today. Today, Vlad is a pastor in Washington and author of many books. One I can recommend is *Break Free How to get free and stay free*.

Nature miracles are something many like to think of as just, well, natural. Not necessarily the will of God. It's just natural when a tornado demolishes one person's house and bounces over its neighbor's house, right? Or is it? Nope. Not in my book. How about when an out-of-control fire terrorized the small Hawaiian town of Lahaina, killing hundreds and burning down everything around an old church but leaves it standing unscathed.

In mid-2023, Maria Lanakila Catholic Church in Lahaina, Hawaii, stood tall after a massacre of wildfires ripped through, leaving thousands of buildings demolished to rubble. Many people took the church's standing as a sign of hope. Buildings on the church premises were demolished but the 1846-year-old structure was untouched. Reverend Monsignor Terrence Watanabe says it was an "incredible miracle" that the church survived even as nearby buildings were destroyed. Watanabe said he believes everyone was shocked to see it still standing. He explained that spiritually, people always try to look for the presence of God in the world, whether it be a rainbow or people's love for one another, but this was a whole other level of God's presence.

No matter what type of miracle and what time in history, we can say without hesitation that miracles are happening today as they did in biblical times.

Varying Opinions

For the longest time, I always felt like I had the character trait that my way was better, and everyone should just agree with me from my father. He was a know-everything kind of guy. I felt like I was alone in that thinking, and it was almost shameful. Until God pointed out to me that I was not alone in this walk and most, if not, all people think that their perspective is accurate and that their way is better than others. And (big AND) it is okay for others to have different perspectives. God didn't create my mind like yours and yours like mine, so why should we think alike. As I age, I begin to see the cracks in my theories and my thinking and have been able to realize that not EVERYTHING I think, say, and do is better than others. I will admit, though I do tend to use my persuasive talents to encourage people to see things my way, I am not always right. I am definitely willing to relent a lot quicker these days.

When faced with conflicting perspectives we can run from them, we can argue them, or we can just agree to disagree and accept that the relationship we have with God is different for everyone. If we can accept that we all serve the same God, why then does it matter how we do it. If it is biblically based and Jesus-driven, who cares how someone else perceives or expresses their opinions. My challenge to you is this. Accept that not everyone is going to see miracles or even God like you do, and let that be okay with you. It's just plain easier.

Jesus Joy

I recently had a friend say being a Christian is boring. I hurt for her because she felt like her old life was fun, and her new life wasn't. Isn't it funny how Satan tries to make us think that the evil things we enjoyed were enjoyable and living a life filled with Jesus isn't. I still dance. I still sing. I still laugh uncontrollably at funny things. I still enjoy a glass of wine or a beer. HOWEVER. I don't striptease. I don't sing inappropriately. I don't take pleasure in things that are harmful. I don't drink alcohol to be drunk. I keep my eyes on Jesus, and as I do that, everything else falls into line.

Evil is easier. It just is. It is easier because we live in a world that encourages a lifestyle that is not Godly. It is easier because we are sinners by nature. It is easier because Satan is constantly working to pull us away from what is good. Having joy over evil may appear hard, but it really is uncomplicated. If we take Satan out of the equation, evil becomes painful, and Jesus becomes our joy.

I am reminded of a childhood song I sang in Sunday school. We'd sing these words and dance and point at our hearts and it still rings true today. "I got the joy joy joy joy down in my heart. Where? Down in my heart to stay." There is something so satisfying about getting to the place in life where you are experiencing Jesus's joy. Joy in everything you do because everything you make points back to His will for you in your life. It is beyond fulfillment. It overflows, it surpasses all that the world has to offer, and it is what Jesus desires for you. I'm praying you receive Jesus's joy in your life starting right now.

Be Patient

Ugh, what? Why? I mean, I just want to groan outwardly right now as I contemplate being patient. I am impatient. I can self-assess myself just fine. I can admit it. I am, from time to time, more times than not impatient. It's in times of intense impatience that I grow more in Christ than I do when I am being patient. When I am weak, he makes me strong. It says in 2 Corinthians 12:8-10 *"Three different times I begged the Lord to take it away. Each time, he said, "My grace is all you need. My power works best in weakness." So now I am glad to boast about my weaknesses so that the power of Christ can work through me. That's why I take pleasure in my weaknesses and in the insults, hardships, persecutions, and troubles that I suffer for Christ. For when I am weak, then I am strong."* These verses speak of a thorn in Paul's flesh that tormented him. I am certain that Paul's pain was more than that of my impatience, but it gives me hope. Because it isn't just physical pain, he is speaking of. He is talking about all that afflicts us. Whatever your pain, whatever your shortcomings, whatever you lack in God says, I got you. So in those moments of impatience, I am reminded of this more than ever now. Gods got me, and my miracle is coming.

My oldest son responded to me when he was just a toddler when I said, "You know what they say about patience". And he said, "I know, I know, Mom, patience will avert you. It was a perfect example of a Freudian slip for sure. It's one that still makes me giggle today. But God does claim patience is a virtue. A very important virtue at that. The virtue of patience combats one of the seven deadly sins: wrath. The more patience we exhibit, the less angry we will be. The less angry we are, the more open we will be, accepting everything in God's timing, not ours. In itself, anger is not a sin; however, anger most definitely leads us astray from God's will in our lives and can certainly lead to sin if we do not control those emotions.

Tiny Miracles

Because everything is so much bigger than karma, it is important for us to see His daily occurrences in our lives as our tiny miracles. I once had a good friend say, "You had a big miracle; I have tiny miracles." I thought that strange, almost humorous, at the time. But when I played everything out from start to finish, God, in His master plan, had to perform a lot of tiny miracles to pull off my "big" miracle. His daily interventions in my life that I don't even know or realize could be simply saving me from something catastrophic. Just recently, every time for a week straight, I left the house, pulled out of my garage, and pushed the garage door button over and over, but nothing. Oh, and then maybe a little movement of the door. I would get out and use the code on the side of the garage, nothing. I would go into the garage and press that button as well, nothing. This would go on for a minimum of 5 minutes until, finally, the garage door would go down. Now impatient me would have been furious, tiny miracle seeker me determined God was keeping me for a reason. What was that reason, I do not know. I do not need to know. I needed to see it as a simple trusting God moment and accept that whatever I was being kept from was for my best interest. I chose to remain calm and pray, and boom, down came the garage door. I could have easily seen this as a frustrating moment. It could have sent me on a path to have a horrible day, but by captivating it, I could understand, this too could be just a tiny miracle. One that I cannot begin to understand, but I can have faith that God knows. What an ah-ha moment, right? I can see anything from this perspective if I choose. Something so small as an extra ten minutes of my time, I can see it as wasted or that it is all just part of His infinite plan. It is very freeing to give that burden to God and not allow life's minors to become majors.

Divine Interventions

Free will is a blessing and a curse. Without miracles or divine intervention, we would all surely be cursed at times. God's divine intervention is in our lives daily. He directs us and leads us down the path of righteousness. The daily crossroads on this path can quickly veer us off that path if we do not stay focused on God's intention in our lives. I personally feel like I need to be kept on a short leash. The more I take over, the more I try and go my own way, the further I feel from His presence. I am reminded of the saying, "Let go and let God." God seeks to show us all His divine interventions in our lives. We need only be open to accepting His role versus ours.

Divine interventions are what the Bible is all about. From beginning to end, every page that turns takes you on the most amazing adventure of God's entrenchment in the lives of His people. As Christians, we should consider ourselves just another chapter in God's most amazing book of life. The bible has been written, and we are living it out today.

CHAPTER 6

Spirit-Filled Peace

"Be Still and know that I am God" Psalm 46:10

I love this verse. I cannot emphasize how much I need to be reminded of this daily! My mindset has been quite contradictory to that verse. I have spent much of my life thinking, sometimes aloud, "Why can't I be on the go and know you are God?" I used to be a go-getter. I used to run myself ragged for my kids, my husband, my family, my friends, my job, my church, and everything before my God. And in that order! You see where I am going with this don't you. I volunteered for everything. I mean everything, and I couldn't understand why I was so exhausted. I couldn't understand why I was overextending myself. I can look back on those times in my life with gratitude because I realize I had to go through those times in my life to appreciate the peace I have now with being still and knowing He is God. This is just another example of Trisha learning the hard way and not just listening to God first.

I did all those things, never really giving much to any of them because I found stretching myself so thinly to exceed expectations that I rarely met them. I can look back today and see that my actions may have hurt some. My actions may have caused me more pain than good because I was rarely still with God. So much that I can remember being in bible study with some ladies and during the prayer, I was writing a mental grocery list of things I needed to pick up on the way home from church. A bible study group I was leading, mind you!!

It has taken me longer than I hope it does you to realize, it isn't about the acceptance of others; it's about His acceptance. When I had that ah-ha moment, it was like a hundred light bulbs going off over my head. I became a Jesus freak from that day forward.

It wasn't to neglect others like a complete contradiction: "To on the go and know God." It was and is to strengthen my connection to the source of where my strength comes from. If I take the time necessary to fill my spirit with peace, I am a more effective, valuable asset to those things I wanted to go get in the first place. In turn, ultimately pleasing others because I please Him first. That in turn, gives you that feeling you were looking for all along just now through the right connections.

Stop Circumventing Christ

I was an aviation electrician in the U.S Navy stationed in Jacksonville, Florida. So let me use what little skills I still have from that amazing time supporting my country and give you a quick connection explanation. Trust me, it will be a very kindergarten-level description here. I am going to give you a quick explanation of an electric circuit.

An electric circuit is a complete circular path in which electric flows. A simple circuit consists of a load, a conductor, and a source. For example, when you turn on your living room light switch, the source is the electricity running into your home for the electric company. The conductor is the light switch, and the load is the light bulb turning on. To be completely honest here, I wasn't even using my source to its full potential the way it was intended. Electricity looks for the path of least resistance by getting to the source the quickest way possible, and I was definitely taking the long path. If I had chosen the path of least resistance originally, I would not have experienced so much short-circuiting throughout my life. Short-circuiting is when electricity flows through an unintended pathway instead of through the circuit. The directions I took in my life to get to where I am was long, a very long circuit that could have easily been circumvented had I chosen the path of least resistance to Christ.

Great news, my loss is your gain. You can stop circumventing Christ by starting at the source and letting all the strength flow from Him. If your connection is loose, tighten it today. Because you never know when Satan will attack, and that short circuit can set your life ablaze. There are probably hundreds of ways to describe this need in your life. I hope that this one has helped you see the need for a direct connection to Christ in your life over all else. But just in case you're a visual person like me here is a diagram to help. Electricity is all about diagrams.

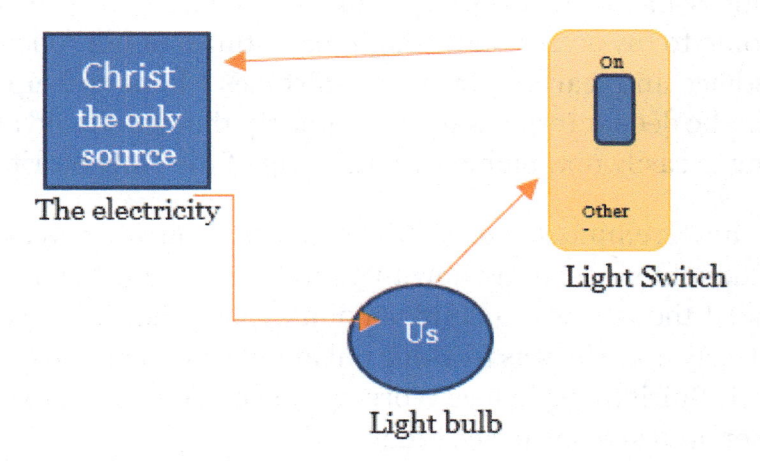

Christ the only source
The electricity

On / **Other**
Light Switch

Us
Light bulb

If we don't put ourselves first in the connection, we are not taking the path of least resistance. Ultimately setting ourselves up to short circuit, and that is just where Satan wants us to do.

It is important to keep the switch in the on position, which closes the circuit, allowing the electricity to flow. Only when we close out all the other things leading us from Christ (i.e., the light switch) and sit still in his presence will we truly be able to experience the spirit-filled peace God intends for us to have throughout our lives.

The Helper

Great news is that God has sent us a helper. Jesus assures us in John 14:26: *"But when the Father sends the Advocate as my representative—that is, the Holy Spirit—he will teach you everything and will remind you of everything I have told you."* If you are somewhere, you can shoot Hallelujah! Do it now! Without the Holy Spirit living in us, can you imagine the challenges we live with every day and how much more complicated they could be?

The way to irrefutable peace that is filled by the Holy Spirit is accepting Jesus as your Lord and Savior. To truly experience happiness and joy in all circumstances is such. I must preface it has come to my attention through many times of not following this advice and learning from the mistakes I hope to help you avoid. The deep interpersonal relationship that we should all be craving is easily obtainable with the help of the Holy Spirit.

I am reminded of the time my now 6-year-old granddaughter asked me how to go to heaven, and I explained in what I thought was a child version explanation; however, it was clearly not. She was freaking out about God in her heart and the Holy Spirit living in her. Worry not, I googled how to explain it to her, and she has peace today.

In my imagination, I see the spirit realm outside of my body and demons constantly attempting to attach themselves to me, in turn misdirecting me and attacking me. I can close my eyes and see the Holy Spirit encompassing me in a bubble and fighting my battles for me. In the background of my imagination the song "Surrounded (Fight My Battles)" by Michael W. Smith playing "This is how I fight my battles; it may look like I am surrounded, I am surrounded by you." Worshiping through music, whether in my imagination or in real life, grounds me and connects me to the Holy Spirit.

Sticking with my electricity analogy. The Holy Spirit is the conduit that connects us to God. A conduit is a protective shell that houses the electric wire that the electricity travels through. While protecting us, the Holy Spirit convicts us of our sins. The spirit guides us, comforts us, bears our burdens with us, enlightens us to our spiritual gifts, instills the desire to obey God, opens our eyes to God words, and encourages to be fervent in our prayer life. The Holy Spirit expands our connection to God by opening our hearts to God and restores us when we fail to be more like Christ in our actions. The Holy Spirit enlightens us on the areas of growth needed in our lives for us to reach maturity as Christians. This enlightenment truly gives that peace that passes all understanding that can and will fill us with contentment.

Be Victorious

Choosing victory even when you do not feel victorious, even when you don't feel peace, is the authority that God gives us through the Holy Spirit. Calling on the Holy Spirit to fight our battles is how we can be victorious and defeat Satan's attacks on our lives. Satan does not want us to be victorious. Satan does not want us to realize the strength that the Holy Spirit offers us. Satan prefers you and I to stay in the dark with as little light as possible. The darkness that keeps us from seeing the truth that sets us free from the bondage he tries to keep us in.

If you are a parent or if you were ever a child, which we can all assume that we were all children, you can remember the times you said or heard, "Don't touch that; it's hot"! Those 5 little words are so ingrained in our psyche that we can be transported back in time to the times we heard those words come from us or our parents. Some of us touched it anyway and learned the hard way. Satan is always going to be that little devil on your left shoulder saying, "Touch it"! I say to you, resisting that urge to believe that little voice and screaming loudly "I

HAVE THE AUTHORITY OVER YOU SATAN." even if you are as oppositional to direction as I am, you won't touch that which is hot. When fear or worry or any kind of pain begins to creep in shout it out. Make sure Satan hears you loud and clear. Jesus spoke specifically on this in the book of Luke.

Luke 10:19 "Look, I have given you authority over all the power of the enemy, and you can walk among snakes and scorpions and crush them. Nothing will injure you."

Jesus goes on to tell us not to rejoice and be boastful of it but to rejoice because our names are registered in heaven. However, while on this earth, we are to carry out his plan for our lives. Those plans include furthering his kingdom and defeating the works of Satan and the power he has over our lives. Satan is worse than the most defiant child. When you give him an inch, he will instantly take a mile. The longer we allow him to be controlling our thoughts and feelings the deeper the bitterness will root itself in our lives. The Holy Spirit desires to ground you with roots so strong in your connection to God that no matter how painful your circumstances you are filled with peace.

Release Your Burdens

I've often imagined a life without burdens. One that is full of peace, harmony, and no conflict. What a utopia that would be right? As I grow older, the realization of just a day of utopia is seriously unlikely. Every moment upon waking, I can expect something is coming at me that could become burdensome. This is not to say as a Christian, I cannot handle it because Hallelujah, I can do all things…. That well-known verse goes on to say that through Christ, who strengthens me, The Holy Spirit will strengthen you and I to get through any burden Satan puts before us if we only give the burden to Christ.

The longer we hold those burdens, the harder it is to let them go. Burdens are painful; they can weigh you down till you cannot even get out of bed due to the fear of how I will get through the pain of this burden again today? The longer we allow it to hang on to us, the more it consumes us. It can become an infestation in our lives that can eat away at the core of who we are. Yes, experiences in life change us. But by releasing the burden of the painful experiences to the Holy Spirit as quickly as we most possibly can, we can regain our strength in who we truly are in Christ.

Imagine it like this. A man walks up to you and says this. "I have a gift beyond your comprehension. A gift so amazing that all of your troubles will be taken away from you and dealt with by another. A gift that only requires you to believe, and it will be so. A gift that will take all your pain and sorrow if you only release it. A gift so valuable, but the price is free because it has already been paid for." Would you turn away from that man offering such an awesome gift? Maybe because you might think it's too good to be true. What if he threw in that the gift also offers everlasting life in utopia? How would you walk away from such an enticing offer like that? That is what God offers through the death on the cross of Christ and the allowing of the Holy Spirit into your heart. You need only accept the gift and keep your eyes on the prize, Beloved.

Peace Beyond Our Understanding

Without the knowledge of what is offered in the bible, the gift has less value. Simply put, the more we read the word of God, the more we turn to the Holy Spirit in our time of need, and the more we experience peace beyond our understanding. Paul said in Philippians 4:7, "Then you will experience God's peace, which exceeds anything we can understand. His peace will guard your hearts and minds as you live in Christ Jesus." Let's unpack this verse for a bit. This verse is telling us don't try to figure it out. You aren't gonna get it. It's beyond our comprehension, but it is magnificent because it is God's peace. When I read this verse, I like to think of the Holy Spirit (our conduit) as a protective shell encompassing me in this perfectly me-shaped bubble, guarding me against it all. My vivid imagination kicks in even further. I visualize Satan throwing everything at me as hard as he can. The Holy Spirit, like Wonder Woman, is throwing up her bracelets of victory to ward off the pain, saving me whilst I chill in my perfect me-shaped God bubble.

Truly, peace is available in all circumstances; that's right ALL circumstances. However, without making the conscious choice to trust God, our bubble will get holes. Each time we choose to deal with fear, worry hurt, and all other pains instead of allowing God to deal with them, the holes will expand larger and larger until we are completely exposed to Satan's schemes. This is seriously Beloved, where the act of free will, I believe, is so pertinent. Free will isn't a one-and-done kind of thing. Free will is what we must submit to God in everything in order for us to truly experience the peace that passes all understanding. Here is a quick prayer to God that will help set you on the path to submitting your free will to Christ in all things.

Father, I am thankful for my free will. I humbly give you my life today to do as you wish. When Satan attempts to attack me in my walk with you, I ask that you remind me of the strength that comes from the Holy Spirit. That I man lean on you for peace in all things and accept your will be done in my life.

Every Aspect

There are certain times in my life when I feel God's presence more than others. There are certain areas in my life where I feel God's presence more than others. God doesn't call us to give

Him the easy parts of our lives. God doesn't call us to give Him the hard parts of our lives either. Because He knows us more intimately than ever, we know ourselves. He calls us to give it all to Him. Every aspect.

It may seem silly, a man reading this may not relate but I am certain you have bore witness to it. I like to think I am not alone in this dilemma, but I can sometimes stand in my closet for a half an hour trying on various outfits and not liking a one. I don't like the way it feels, or the way I look in it. Sometimes it hugs the wrong places or makes me feel fat. When this happens, I have to stop and pray. *"God, you've got this. I know I am wonderful made by you, and though this is a minor, I am making it a major. Please help me find contentment in the clothes I am about to put on."* As soon as I give it to Him, I immediately find peace in what I put on next. It is a little thing. However, because God desires a relationship with us, I take comfort in those moments that this, too is just an aspect of my life He desires to be involved in. And the quicker I get that prayer done, the quicker my holes in my bubble can be repaired and I no longer feel the negative opinions of myself that Satan is using to attack me with. This is how minimal of an aspect we need to include God in. He desires to be in every aspect of our lives. Giving the Holy Spirit access to all areas of our lives allows us the opportunity to experience the fullness of peace that God intends for us.

Building on Peace

Certain aspects come easily; however, some do not. What is an easy aspect for you might not be easy for me. A positive way to build on your peace is by asking yourself what fruits of the spirit are hardest for me to allow the Holy Spirit to work through me. This is a self-check that we should all be doing quite regularly because situations change as our lives evolve, and though peace may be a challenge in one situation, it may be simple in another. Galatians 5:22-23 is where you can find this verse. *"But the Holy Spirit produces this kind of fruit in our lives:* **love, joy, peace, patience, kindness, goodness, faithfulness, gentleness, and self-control.** *There is no law against these things!"* Let's take comfort in knowing when we are weak; we can call on the Holy Spirit to fill us with the fruits we are lacking at that time.

It is important for us to build on the mindset of peace because the world is constantly working against us. It is constantly working to steal our peace. Without choosing the Holy Spirit to fill us with peace, accepting and spotting miracles in our lives will be arduous.

These Three Things

Obedience. Gratitude. Contentment.

Without choosing these actions in our lives, achieving spirit-filled peace is a pipe dream. Let's review each of them.

Obedience is defined as compliance with authority. When you accept Jesus as your savior, you have put Him in a position of authority over your life. If you were like me, you cried out in shame and begged Him to take your pain because you didn't want to handle it any longer. In doing this, we are saying you are the head where you lead, I will follow. Have you ever tried to walk backward for any length of time? Well, if you haven't don't try it because sooner or later you will trip and fall. With God as our head, we are the body. The body should follow where the head leads, right? Being obedient to God implies surrender. Where you lead Lord, I will follow, even when I don't understand. Even when it hurts and even when I don't want to. Obedience is not perfection. God has zero expectations of you or me to be perfect. Can I get an AMEN! God does call us to strive to be the best we can possibly be every day in every situation. The Greek version of Ephesians 5:1 says *"Become ye therefore imitators of God."*

Gratitude is defined as readiness to show appreciation. To show true gratitude, you must be willing to be humble. How many times a day do we say thank you and put very little thought into it? Thank you without humility is not true gratitude. An example of true gratitude is the one Samaritan leper who was one of ten that Jesus healed. After following Jesus's request by going to the priests to show them he was healed from leprosy, he turned around and trekked back to Jesus to say "Praise God" as he fell to the ground at Jesus's feet thanking him for what he had done for him. That is 10% of the lepers Jesus healed. Are you part of the 10%? Do you thank him in everything. It is a conscious choice we must try and make to be grateful in every area whether it is something that is as amazing as a miracle healing or as small as your car engine turning over as you turn the key in the ignition. Everything you and I have is because God has given it to us. By making it your mission to find gratitude in all things you can find peace that brings about immense joy.

Contentment is defined as feeling satisfaction. Paul is an amazing example of contentment in Philippians 4:11; he states that he is never in need as he has learned to be content with whatever he has. Paul was a true visionary in his time. The miracles and work that God performed through Paul can be mind-boggling. Though I have no intentions on limited God I can assume that this book will be read mostly by Americans. We as Americans, have so much more than other countries. We are already blessed beyond measure. This is not to say you shouldn't strive for better in your life. Only that to achieve spirit-filled peace, we must find contentment in all circumstances in our lives. Even when we think it is too big, too hard, or too painful, we must be content with knowing our problems are not too big of a problem for God. Truly, how vain we must be to think our problems are bigger than HIM!

FOCUS FOCUS FOCUS

I once went on a wellness weekend getaway with a friend of mine and spent the entire time complaining. The first thing we did when we got there was yoga poses in the dark. The next day was filled with healthy eating and detoxing, along with tons of water drinking. My friend was so elated to share this experience with me, and I spent every second possible pointing out all the things from a negative perspective. Though it was a fun experience, being wrapped in plastic with essential oils on my body while I had to pee like crazy was not relaxing in any way whatsoever to me. To be fair to myself, I did try to approach my negative comments from a humorous perspective, making light of everything, but it was negative, nonetheless. Afterwards my friend pretty much was no longer my friend. She asked me to come to her home for a chat, and she informed me that she was no longer interested in being close to me because I had brought her down. She needed positive people in her life. Though I tried to reason with her by apologizing and things were never the same, and we never hung out again. It really hurt. It was a huge learning experience for me. I didn't want to be someone who was considered negative. I set out to change that about myself. I would like to say I am positive all the time now, but to be completely honest, that wouldn't be true. Being positive about situations does not come naturally for me. I have to remind myself to focus on the positives. When I start to see ole negative Nelly rear her ugliness, I squash it by replacing it with a positive thought or statement. The more I focus on the positives in my life, the more I have peace. The more peace I have, the more positive things seem to be. I want to have a joyful heart, not a crushed spirit. I desire to encourage and support others through my joyful heart. You should want that for yourself as well. There are so many things going on in this world around us that is negative it is sometimes hard to do that is why it is so important to focus on the positives God has blessed you with. Even when it's hard to see them through the negatives, they are all around us!

Stomp on Satan

When my youngest daughter was little, she would stomp her feet, cross her arms in front of herself, and just make the cutest little face to inform us of her disapproval. I believe I have photos as proof. Though she is in her 20's now, she still does it from time to time, however, it lacks the cuteness that came with her toddler years. Stomping is an act of treading heavily, and it typically comes with anger. It insinuates frustration and strength. The muscle you use to stomp is the quadricep, the muscle in the front of your thigh. Only second to the jaw muscle known as the masseter muscle, the quadricep is considered the strongest muscle. It is comprised of four (quad) muscles intertwined and overlapping to release great force. Have you ever watched a crime movie? In nearly every movie you have someone kicking in doors with the strength of one kick. Have you ever watched traditional wine-making stomping of the grapes? The strength and weight of the stomping releases the juices and begins fermenting. In Psalms 110:1, David writes of God speaking to Jesus: *"Sit in the place of honor at my right hand until I humble your enemies, making them a footstool under your feet."* Do not forget Satan is your enemy, and while Jesus sits at the right hand of God today until His return, it is our duty as Christians filled with the Holy Spirit to make Satan our footstool. We are not to allow Satan even a foothold. Ephesians 4:26-27 *"Don't sin by letting anger control you...for anger gives a foothold to the devil."* So when you are facing something that creates anger in you, cross your heart to protect it and stomp out that anger on Satan, but smile because you have the peace of the Holy Spirit.

Just Breathe

My good buddy book of Job has quite a bit of breathing through out it. I can only imagine in his struggles that he had to do a lot of breathing to calm his soul. In Job 12:10, Job says, *"For the life of every living thing is in His hand and the breath of every human being."* It is hard to fathom that God knows every breath we take. I feel like I need to break out in song again. The Police song from back in 1983. *"Every Breath You Take"* could just as easily be a song from God. I won't bore you with more song lyrics just yet, but go have a listen, and you'll see what I mean. Breathing is as natural as blinking and swallowing. We just do it because that is by His design. We don't even have to think about it to do it. But when you are looking for a spirit-filled peace in your life, it helps to take the time to be intentional about your breathing.

It helps to slow your subconscious mind, and it gives your heart a chance to slow down. Meditating on a word, phrase, or bible verse can bring about a sense of calmness that enables the Holy Spirit to work in you to bring you the peace you need in that moment. I personally just say "Jesus" over and over between my breaths. There is nothing that calms my soul more than the word Jesus. Take a second right now, close this book and close your eyes, and deep breathe; feel your chest rise as you inhale and exhale the magnificent word Jesus for a hot minute. Just let the Holy Spirit work in and through you to fill you full of the peace that only Jesus Christ can provide for you.

CHAPTER 7

Confidence Comes with Christ

20/20 God Vision

When you look in the mirror, how do you see yourself? Do you see all your little imperfections, or do you see yourself as God sees you? In today's world, where everywhere you turn on social media, it is all about looks and body image; it is important to look through God's googles instead of Satan's sight.

How precious are God's words in Psalms 139:13-16 where David speaks of how much effort God put into you and I. *"You made all the delicate, inner parts of my body and knit me together in my mother's womb. Thank you for making me so wonderfully complex! Your workmanship is marvelous—how well I know it. You watched me as I was being formed in utter seclusion, as I was woven together in the dark of the womb. You saw me before I was born. Every day of my life was recorded in your book. Every moment was laid out before a single day had passed."* When I look in the mirror, I must admit I am challenged to see His marvelous workmanship. It is hard for me to see myself as perfectly as God sees me. Part of having 20/20 God vision is truly looking past the outward appearance and seeing into your soul and the souls of those around you. This is truly the parts that God cares about and desires to strengthen you to see better, not your wrinkles, your scars, your hairline, your large nose, or no upper lip. Look in the mirror and see past all that to the soul that will leave the wrinkly, scared, bald, big nose, no upper lip self behind and rise up to stand before the Lord someday. That is what He desires most for you. Another part of that 20/20 God vision is accepting yourself and the flaws of others as the ways that make us unique. Not one person on this planet has experienced life as I have in its entirety so how could they possibly compare. Every second of our lives is part of God's plan. He knows what we are going to do before we do. That kind of realization is meant to give us confidence and should release us of any fears. It should give us strength to know that His vision for us is clear. One of the most often quoted verses in the bible is Jeramiah 29:11 typically it is used to encourage people in their finances because he has a plan for them to prosper. The next phrase in that verse is sometimes overlooked or underappreciated, and that is "Not to harm you." That is his vision for us all. Why, then, does harm come to us, you ask? It is the question of the ages. Ultimately God's plan is out of our scope of knowledge. Harm may come to you or me because of many things whether it be our free will and choices we make, or it may be even bigger than that. The death of a loved one, a car accident that changes the trajectory of your life, to writing a book you never in a million years thought you would be writing, these are things that only God in His infinite wisdom comprehends. Could the death of one bring life to another? Could the pain of a car accident set you on a totally different path for Christ like it has me? Or could you, the reader of this book right now, be spiritually growing? His vision is far beyond our scope of understanding; however, we can strive to understand. All along, we trust in His choices because we are confident in His word that He has plans not to harm us. Truly, I cannot emphasize this enough: even when we do not see Him working, He is, and it is always for our good. Remind yourself that all things are meant to further the kingdom of God. That Beloved is what 20/20 God vision looks like.

Christ Like Confidence

We are called to have the same attitude as Christ. My first tattoo as an adult was Isaiah 40:31 it is on my right wrist. Not the whole verse, of course, just the book chapter and page; the whole verse would have needed a larger space for sure.

But those who trust in the Lord will find new strength.
They will soar high on wings like eagles.
They will run and not grow weary.
They will walk and not faint.

These words give me the strength and the confidence that I need in Christ that I can be strong in my convictions. It is my very favorite verse. Isaiah is the most significant Old Testament prophet of Jesus. When I think of this verse I like to consider Jesus as the new strength Isaiah was speaking about. Jesus had and will always have the strength of both humans and God. Being the only sinless being to ever walk this earth. It boggles my mind when I think of the confidence Christ must have had. Imagine if you had the ability to go without sin your entire life. How arrogant that would make us, but not Jesus. He was humble and kind, always exhibiting all the fruits of the spirit. Imagine the confidence you would have knowing God's plan and still being in a human body. The confidence that comes with that knowledge living inside you had to be an amazing feeling. This is what we are called to have. A confidence in ourselves and our relationship with God that no matter what we see before us, no matter how horrible our situation might be, God has a beautiful future that is beyond our wildest dreams. Whether the future is here on earth or in heaven, it means no difference because, ultimately, we are called to have that confidence like Christ.

Self Worth & Self Confidence

It is easy to say we should have confidence in Christ, but that is easier said than done. Many of us have had pasts that have led us to feel unworthy. Many of us struggle with the pain of mistakes that have led us to addictions, failed relationships, financial struggles, and so on.

Have you ever heard the saying, "It takes a village to raise a child?" It takes only one to dilute a child's self-worth and self-confidence.

Overcoming the challenges of the past is no easy task, and I want to encourage you that no matter where you are in life, God loves you and desires to bring you to a place of confidence in yourself. Here are a couple of practical ways you can do this, in turn opening your mind up to a closer connection to Christ and ultimately opening your eyes to miracles.

Know God's Promises

Many are unsure of what God's promises truly are for us, and without that knowledge, it is difficult to overcome the doubt Satan puts in our minds on a daily basis (when we allow him, of course). The Bible is very specific on God's promises to us, we need only seek out those promises and begin to accept with great conviction each of them. Here are but a few of God's promises to you and me.

Another one of my favorite verses, Romans 8:28, is clear that all, not just some or just the ones we cherry-pick for God, but ALL things work together for the good of those that are called according to his purpose. That is huge, Beloved, enormous. When we stand on this promise alone, we can build courage in ourselves. This promise is a doozy and is instrumental in inspiring self-confidence.

Pinpoint Your Confidence Killers

We all have things in our lives that bring us down, and those things Satan revels in. He loves to expand your confidence, killers. Some examples of confidence killers are control, money, achievements, pleasure, or people. Let's start with control. I like control, and I don't know very many people that don't like control. Jesus was quoted in Luke 9:24 as saying, *"If you try to hang on to your life, you will lose it. But if you give up your life for my sake, you will save it."* Did you read that? "Give up your life for my sake!!!" I interpret that as giving up your desires and, in turn, giving up control. When we try to control situations, the devil loves it. There have literally been times in my life when I am 100% certain God is just up there shaking his head at me, saying, "Look, there she goes, trying to do it on her own again!" We think that if we control it, we can be confident, but ultimately, it puts us right where the devil wants us: out of sync with Christ.

Money: Ugh! What a killer money can be to our confidence. If we don't have enough, or someone else has more, or the thought that all we need is just a little bit more, then we will be happy. Money is truly one of the biggest challenges we face in today's society. It, unfortunately, is a necessary evil, and success is sadly determined by how much you have from a worldview. However, we are called to have a biblical perspective, and in 1 Timothy 6:17 Paul called money unreliable and encourages us to trust that God will provide all that we need. When we are without money, we begin to lack confidence in God and in ourselves, which in turn lessens our self-worth.

Achievements: I am a Gen X'er. I hate to say it, but our generation was the last of the generations that didn't get a trophy for just showing up. We had to achieve everything we got, or well, we just didn't get it. In part, that is a blessing because it causes us to appreciate the things we have achieved; however, it can also lead to pride. Pride is what got Lucifer thrown out of heaven y'all. I'm just sayin'.... that, pride is a sin you just don't want to get wrapped up in because you may feel confident, but it's really a killer. Achievements, if not properly directed to the source of our success just bring the devil so much joy. All your successes are to be given to God for the glory. It may seem like you've done something of your own strength, but He is the one who gave you that strength. This is not to say you cannot find your self-worth in the achievements, only that the more you offer praise to God because He is the source, will you truly build Christ-like confidence.

Pleasure: Solomon, known today for his wisdom and riches, said plain and simple. *"I looked at everything I had worked so hard to accomplish; it was all so meaningless—like chasing the wind. There was nothing really worthwhile anywhere."* Ecclesiastes 2:11. When we seek earthly pleasures, we get earthly results, when we seek heavenly pleasures, we get heavenly results. Pleasure, though it feels good in the moment like Solomon said, is like chasing the wind. When we focus on what gives us earthly pleasures, we spend our lives running the hamster wheel and our confidence will die slowly with every complete turn of the wheel. When we focus on what gives us heavenly pleasures, God builds up our self-worth in Him, and we feel the confidence with every step we take all along, drawing us nearer to Christlike confidence.

People: This is by far the BIGGEST confident killer I have experienced in my lifetime. As I write these words, I accept my confession is to follow. I have spent a great deal of my life seeking approval from relationships in my life. I have spent far too long of my life seeking men to fulfill my needs instead of going to the source of living water. My alter has been people. My confidence has been rooted in the approval of others for far too long. People have been whom I turned to for my self-worth, and when I no longer felt worthy of them, I discarded them without hesitations or thoughts. Once I realized where my worth truly came from, I was able to find exponential growth through Christ alone and love myself through him. This epiphany completely altered the way I related to people and, in turn, loved them in a way I never understood. This confession was my confidence killer. If it is yours, I hope that my confession encourages you to seek Christ's approval in your life.

Choosing Christ over people was truly the only way I was able to realize my self-worth.

Mess to Message

I love this phrase. Let God turn your mess into a message. As a child sitting in a Southern Baptist church pew, I could have never imagined I would someday be writing a book confessing my mess. I was raised in the South with the understanding that as long as people didn't see it, it didn't happen. Miranda Lambert said it best in her song "Mama's Broken Heart" when she sang.

> *"Word got around to the barflies and the Baptists.*
> *My mama's phone started ringin' off the hook.*
> *I can hear her now sayin' she ain't gonna have it.*
> *Don't matter how you feel, only matters how you look.*
> *Go and fix your makeup girl, it's just a breakup.*
> *Run and hide your crazy and start actin' like a lady.*
> *Cause I raised you better, gotta keep it together."*

I do not blame Miranda's mom or my own for this upbringing. It was a different time, and it was how they were raised. But there is something so freeing about letting go of your mess and showing your truth to others so that they not only do not feel like the only ones struggling but also that God gives us grace when we fail. Furthermore, we don't have to be perfect. That we will not be sin free upon accepting Jesus and most importantly that we are forgiven for it all. James makes it pretty clear in 5:16 *"confess your sins to each other."* As not to use this out of context he was speaking specifically about praying for each other. Which leads to the next point, how can we get prayers from others if we are so worried about what they are thinking about us. Declaring our mess is liberating and shows Satan he does not have dominion over our lives. Satan loves to see you and I struggling with confession. He revels in knowing we are hiding our faults away in pride. Liberating yourself is a form of confidence you can only get from Christ.

Shame can be a dirty word in our vocabulary if we let it. Shame can cause us to experience an undeniable lack of confidence. The more shame we have the more likely the distance from our true connection to Christ. Jesus suffered an unimaginable death on the cross for you and I to be shame free. Accepting our short comings and failures in life and turning them into something that furthers the kingdom for Christ is how we can pay homage to Jesus's sacrifice for us. Humbling ourselves in our messes and turning them into a message is freeing to us. Imagine if you will each mistake as a pound of weight on your body. I personally would be found starring in an episode of TLC's show my 600lb Life if that were the case. Now imagine having weight loss surgery and waking up with not only no pain but weighing your ideal weight. That is the freedom Christ's sacrifice gives us. The shackles Satan tries to keep us in with the shame of our mistakes can be lifted by being confident of Christ's gift over our lives. Using our messes is one of the most powerful tools we have to help others in their walk with Jesus. Make every effort in your search for being open to miracles to let go of your shame and use it for God's good.

Be a Liver

I have known Jesus my whole life. I have been a lover of Jesus since I can remember, or so I thought. I have not been a liver for Jesus my whole life. I spent most of my life with one and a half feet in the world and half a foot in my walk with God. I teetered on the proverbial typical hypocritical Christian correlations that many nonbelievers like to reference when referencing Christians. If someone was asked, "Is Trisha a Christian?" I do not think they would respond with a resounding "Yes!" At best, I believe others would have responded with an "I don't know!" Whether my heart was in it or not, my actions didn't portray that. You can love Jesus, and you can even say you love Jesus, but your actions will always speak louder than your words. I wasn't living Jesus, so then the question I had to ask myself was if your actions aren't showing you are a believer, are you really a believer? If you truly have a heart for Christ, then why are you ashamed? Why are you not living out your truth and showing it off like a badge of honor? After my car accident, I saw so much more in a different light. I saw what God's truth really looked like in my life and how honored I should be to not only confess my faith but to live it out for His glory. That transition from riding the fence with 1 ½ feet in the world and ½ a foot in with Christ changed dramatically. I pray that my miracle story can move you. If only one step closer to being all in for Jesus. This movement of not be ashamed but being boldly proud of your connection to Christ is pivotal for being confident in him and being more receptive to miracles.

Listening to the Right Voice

Are you listening to HIS voice or HELL'S voice? Sometimes, it is difficult to decipher whether something is from God or from Satan. There are a few ways to effectively determine this. It is mandatory we get this right for a deeper connection to Christ and to ultimately have confidence in Christ.

One way to determine if it is from God is to turn to God. Turning to God means seeking out His answers in the word. The bible is the best how-to manual out there. Kay Arthur a well-known author and bible teacher has a neat way of determining somethings validity in Christ. She encourages us through her teaching to do what she calls as giving it the "Philippian Frisk." She suggests you ask yourself the question based on Philippians 4:8 whether it is true, noble, right, pure, lovely, admirable, excellent, or praiseworthy. This frisking she inspires us with is meant to help with mindset. Paul encourages us to have the right frame of mind through this verse, but I'd like to encourage you to frisk it coming in just as much as frisking it as it is going out. In other words, if something doesn't have these attributes, plain and simple, it isn't from God. Now, who's to say Satan can't do these things well? I personally believe he can. I believe he is the master of all evil. Though his intention is always rooted in evil, that does not mean Satan can't attempt to use positives to bring about ultimately a negative in your life. Are you wondering now, "Well then, what do I do about that?" Beloved, you pray. You pray for contentment. The devil can not bring about a spirit of contentment in your life like having confidence in Christ does. That restless heart feeling subsides within seconds when you pray for contentment over something if it has been properly frisked. The best part is that anxiety and heart-fluttery feelings don't return if it is God's will. If it keeps coming around and you're still feeling a pull to those voices. The voices that are leaving you with feelings of uncertainty, then chances are at roughly (sarcasm intended) 100% that you are listening to the wrong voice. Here is a quick prayer I toss up daily to God on this topic.

Father, help me discern your will in this situation.
I want to listen to your voice over every other. Please give me the contentment I need to know this is
your will and if
it is not your will, close the door on it and take my desires for it away. In your Holy Name AMEN.

Gotta Have Faith

Everyone is familiar with the saying, "Don't count your chickens before they hatch." It is a commonly used statement to imply that one should not overoptimistically assume something is definite until it happens. This fable has been around for over 2500 years. It was first accounted for in "The Milkmaid and Her Pail" written by an ancient Greek slave named Aesop. Little did Aesop know that his insightful words would stand the test of time.

Proverbs 27:1 is even sometimes referenced as similar. It reads, *"Do not brag about tomorrow since you don't know what the day will bring."* Other versions use the word boast instead of brag.

I say to you, COUNT YOUR CHICKENS! God wants you to have the upmost faith in Him. That is not to say outwardly boast that teeters on pride, however, to have internal satisfaction. Satisfaction that your relationship with Christ produces the kind of faith that you can count your chickens before they hatch. Paul says it quite plainly in Hebrews 11:1 *"Faith shows the reality of what we hope for, it is the evidence of things we cannot see."* Sounds pretty much like the explanation of counting your chickens, doesn't it.

Faith isn't an easy thing to possess. For some people, it comes more easily than for others, but no one is born having faith. There are several reasons why faith is difficult. Here are a few.

Faith requires giving up control. Trusting God with things that we feel like are better handled by us. I sometimes think, "Oh, I don't want to bother God with such little things!" I like to tell myself this to excuse away my inability to relinquish complete control, but God says give it ALL to me and don't try and lean on your own understanding.

Faith requires a spiritual eye. Stop looking for answers and allow God to bring about a clear vision. This goes back to being impatient. Stop looking at things with a sense of anticipation and allow God to show you in His time not your own timing. If you look straight ahead and begin to stare at an object the surroundings begin to blur. The more you hyper-focus, the bigger, brighter, and more detailed the object becomes. Whilst everything else around you becomes the opposite. Having a spiritual eye means you are hyper-focusing on the source and seeing all that the source (God) has to show you. All along letting everything else have less of your time and attention.

Faith requires not knowing the outcome. Have you ever attempted a trust fall? You know the person stands in front of another and falls back expecting the person in the back to catch them? To be honest, I haven't. I don't even know if I have it in me to attempt it. Even with my husband, whom I trust more than anyone, not sure I could do it. But I tell you what if Jesus was doing trust falls, I'd be the first in line. Because even though I do not know with certainty the outcome my faith in Him is that He would catch me no matter what. He will catch you, too, and that is what is required to have true faith.

I am reminded of two songs that I think intertwined would be an awesome tune. The first is the one my granddaughter comes home singing after Sunday school. "My God Is So Big" by Cedarmont Kids goes a little something like this.

My God is so great, so strong and so mighty,

Theres nothing my God cannot do.

Coupled with some "Gotta Have Faith" by George Michael from his first solo debut album. "Faith"!

Cause I gotta have faith

Ooh, I gotta have faith

Because I gotta have faith, faith, faith

I gotta have faith, faith, faith.

You singing it in your head? I sure am. Smashing these two songs together might not be a hit single. But doing it in your heart can bring about Grammy award winning moments in your life. Guaranteed!

Follow Through

I am a starter of things. I have claimed over my life for far too long that I am not a finisher. I'd describe myself as an idea person, good at delegating and encouraging but not actually being the doer. I believe God gave me these character attributes for a reason. I, however, have learned, sometimes the hard way over the years, that if I don't follow through on something for God the first time, he will just keep on keeping on me until I do.

This book is my biggest reference point today, for sure. Without God's continued poking and prodding at my soul I do not think these words would be written for you to be reading this very moment. I can look back at the timeline from my car accident to today and see so many missed opportunities this book could have had during the COVID pandemic had I only listened to His prompting and followed through on His plan. My faith, however, gives me strength, knowing everything is truly in His timing even when I don't know the outcome. Rest assured that if God starts something, no matter how hard you try to push it back to Him, He will see it through to the end. Not only will He finish the plans He has for you and your life, but He will undeniably finish everything He plans until Christ's return. Philippians 1:6 reads, *"And I am certain that God who began the good work within you, will continue His work until it is finally finished on the day when Christ Jesus returns."* I realize this is Paul talking to the Philippians nearly 2000 years ago, but if Paul was certain, um, well you and I should be certain also don'tcha think?

The whole point being made here is you can run, but you cannot hide. You might as well follow through on the things the first time God brings something to your attention, or He will just keep bringing it to you over and over until you get it right. You can be confident in that for sure.

Little Miss/Mr. Do It All

There is a series of books appropriate for 5–7-year-old kids call the Little Miss books and the Mr. Men books. They are small and easy to read and encourage children to be helpful towards others. My daughters during that age had their favorites, one preferred *Little Miss Sunshine* and the other *Little Miss Messy*. Out of pure concern for myself, I will refrain from pointing out which child preferred which, but if you had known them at that age, you'd have been able to guess who liked which book.

As Christians, we tend to feel the pressure to do it all a lot of the time. Serve here, serve there, join this group, lead this group, volunteer here, volunteer there, pray for this need, encourage this person. It can be very fulfilling and an ego boost to be doing all those things for the kingdom of God. That is what we are called to do, are we not? Further, the kingdom of God? Yes, a resounding yes would be the answer to that question. However, not and I repeat, NOT at the expense of your relationship with Christ. Without you making the commitment and the choice to connect with Christ over being the Little Miss/Mr. do it all; feeling confident in Christ will be a hard stretch to reach.

It boils down to flying with a child and needing oxygen on a plane metaphor. If you are flying on a plane and the oxygen masks come flying down in your face because the oxygen levels are of concern you are advised to put on your mask and then your child's mask not the other way around. This is because you could pass out, and then both you and your child would be at risk. Treat your relationship with God in the exact same way, and you will always be filled with the breath of life and you will be able to fulfill God's desires for you in you life.

Acts of service are of the utmost importance because they strengthen our character and, in some cases, humble us (depending on the act of course). As I mentioned in the previous section, some of the attributes that God gave me include being an ideas person, good at delegating and organizing the troops, and enc ouraging them to follow through. These are my gifts. These gifts are from God. Better defined these gifts are just something you are good at doing. No matter what those gifts may be we are to use them for God's good. 1 Peter 4:10 says, *"God has given each of you a gift from his great variety of spiritual gifts. Use them well to serve one another."*

The real kicker here is that many of us tend to do too much or don't use our God-given talents, and we get burnt out. When we are doing all the things that have been encouraged within this chapter, and we are doing the things God has asked of us, we can be 100% confident in Christ. It is through that confidence God will bring about amazing connections for you in your everyday life to bear witness to so much of His miraculous goodness. We need only be open to it all.

CHAPTER 8

Feeling God's Presence

Experiencing Enlightenment

It is like a rude awakening to be able to truly feel and experience enlightenment. Enlightenment is achieving clarity to the degree that you experience peace and joy. This peace and joy lead to breaking the bondage that comes from our self-afflicted suffering. It is feeling like you have truly reached a point in your existence where you have transformed your thoughts and feelings. It is understanding things from an entirely different perspective than what comes naturally. What comes naturally is the me mentality. The mentality that screams out I know what is best for me and what I think is right. But I say this to you, enlightenment will only come when you accept the God mentality, not the me mentality. If you are spending your days focusing on how to get through the next 24 hours on your own, I say to that God's presence isn't overpowering your me mentality. It is at this very moment I am reminded of the 150-year-old hymn written by Horatio Spafford, *"It is Well with my Soul."* Spafford wrote this hymn after the tragedy of losing all four of his daughters when their ship sank in the Atlantic Ocean. How can one have so much fortitude in such a painful time in their life as to write the words *"whatever my lot, though, has taught me to know, it is well it is well with my soul?"* Listen to that song in its entirety with the knowledge you now have, and reach out to me and tell me that it doesn't scream God mentality. I choose to surmise that it was the clarity of peace that can only come from experiencing a profound connection to God that led those lasting words to be written by Mr. Spafford.

Try conceptualizing enlightenment as a deep spiritual awakening or a reckoning to the degree that you can say without a doubt that your life has been changed. This deep soul revival comes with surrendering yourself completely to Jesus Christ. Experiencing enlightenment is a spiritual transformation of our vision of how we see the world and how we see our eternity. Imagine if you will living a life with so much focus and so much understanding that you have complete perspicuity and are awed by your connection to Jesus Christ daily. This is the desire God has for you. This is a oneness with the Holy Spirit living inside of you. Once someone accepts Jesus Christ into their heart and begins living a Christ-centered life, this is what we should all be aspiring to achieve. We all must strive to have that connection where you can attest that you feel God's presence in your life. Paul talks about this in the beginning of Ephesians; he states, *"I pray that the eyes of your heart may be enlightened in order that you may know the hope to which he has called you, the riches of his glorious inheritance in His holy people."* (1:18 NIV) Many people live their whole Christian lives reading that verse and never achieving what Paul is talking about.

There are so many reasons why we hold back from believing that there is nothing greater than God. These reasons stem from a laundry list of attempts that Satan makes to sidetrack our feelings, our thoughts, and our every movement in life. Being a strong-willed person, I tend to lean towards being a bit stubborn and maybe even a wee bit defiant from time to time. Now, you might be reading this and saying this doesn't apply to me; I am not strong-willed. I ask you to indulge me a bit here because I believe we are all a bit strong-willed if we really dive deep into our desires and wants out of this life. It might not be your go-to description of yourself, but ask yourself this. Do I fight for what I think is right, or do I let obstacles get the best of me? Do I crave everything to go the way I think it should go?

I find that being honest with who I am and accepting that this is how God made me and He loves me just as I am, that I don't feel the need to put a veil over the real me. If you take nothing away from this whole book, I pray you take this one piece, and that is that God desires the real you. The real me, being strong-willed, can grapple with the world and Satan's attempts to sidetrack me and my walk with Christ, or I can wrestle against God's presence in my life. There really are no other options. It boils down to the simplicity of good versus evil, darkness versus light. Ponder than for a hot second. Do you truly believe at the depths of your soul that there is nothing greater than God, or are there limitations to this belief in your life? If you did not answer with an astounding, maybe even a shouting out from your soul, "Yes, I believe there is nothing greater," then read on because you CAN feel God's presence in your life, and with every word I write I want to continue to encourage you that there is NOTHING GREATER THAN GOD. **ABSOLUTELY NOTHING!**

Engage Your Senses

Let's look at it from a sensor perspective for a moment. God encourages us through His word and through Paul's teachings in 1 Corinthians and possibly Hebrews (whether he wrote Hebrews or not is questionable) to tap into our senses. Paul flat out told the church of Corinth, *"Come back to your senses as you ought and stop sinning."* (15:34 NIV) Now, let me first say Paul was a little harsh, and though I have been known to be a bit abrasive, I am going to encourage you with a tad bit more kindness today. To draw nearer to God and ultimately feel His presence, there are some senses that we can tap into. Number one, HEARING. Praying to God as if He hears you seems like a simple task, right? If you were saying the same things over and over in your prayer life, a repetitious prayer, if you will, does God really need to be listening? I mean, He is God; He isn't going to forget your prayer. Jesus made it pretty clear in Matthew 6:7 (NKJV) when He said, *"And when you pray do not use vain repetitions as the heathen do."* If you speak to Him with humility in your heart and a foundational belief that He is listening, you begin to draw nearer to Him in a relational way. Listening on our side is a whole different ball of wax. Wow, using that statement "ball of wax" made me feel old and even older when I looked it up and found that it was first used in 1832. Forgive my ADD moment there. Within Proverbs 3:5-12 (MSG) says, *"Listen for God's voice in everything you do, everywhere you go; he's the one who will keep you on track."* You might be thinking right now, this lady is crazy; she's still hearing voices. Some people might actually hear God audibly, but I do not. I feel Him. I feel Him at the core of my being and that is another sense, TOUCH. Feelings are considered an emotional state of reaction. Feelings can also be defined as a sensation like a brief chill on your body or obviously pain.

I have a memory of being somewhere in my early 20s, and two close friends of mine had hurt me so badly that I was heartbroken, bedridden, depressed beyond all measure and I spoke with my father, and he reminded me that vengeance is God's. He realized that every time he let go of the wrongdoings that others did to him and gave it to the Lord that, God always made it known to him of things that transpired where God was taking His vengeance on those that had hurt him. That moment in time gave me peace, not because I had hope for vengeance but because of my experience afterward. It was that night as a non-practicing Christian that I felt the most warming sense of peace come over my whole body; it was like I was being enveloped in this sheer immeasurable love, and I felt what I would now say was the hand of God on my left shoulder. I can close my eyes and almost feel it again nearly 30 years later. That touch was something that altered the trajectory of my life, and it has taken this long to see it. Praise God He doesn't give up on us. Can I get an Amen?!

Another sense that we all desire to engage when feeling His presence is SEEING. Seeing is believing, is it not? To use our site to feel God's presence looks something like this: Have you ever woke up early morning to the most vibrant colors in the sky, and the beauty of that sunrise just puts a smile on your face at how peaceful and relaxing that appears? When we take those moments as little gifts from God, it brings out a connection to God and ultimately, we become closer to Him for it. The sunrise is, of course, only a common example of the many gifts God provides for us daily; we need only keep looking for them and being open to seeing with unabated clarity. Paul brings up in the love chapter in 1 Corinthians 13:12 (MSG) something that may sometimes be overlooked in that chapter and that is *"We don't yet see things clearly. We're squinting in a fog, peering through mist. But it won't be long before the weather clears and the sun shines bright! We'll see it all then, see it all as clearly as God sees us, knowing Him directly just as He knows us!"*

The more we tap into our senses, the more we become spiritually mature. I love the book of Hebrews. Not only because you can make the goofy "He Brews" coffee joke, either. One reason is I like short books of the Bible that I can read in one sitting and feel like I have accomplished much during my time in the Word. However, the book also encourages us to stay faithful to Jesus even through hard times. The one verse that got me in Hebrews regarding this topic was Hebrews 5:14 (AMP) *"But solid food is for the {spiritually} mature, whose senses are trained by practice to distinguish between what is morally good and what is evil."* The pivotal portion of that verse is *"whose senses are trained by practice."* If we want to achieve spiritual maturity, we need to train our senses, ergo feeling His presence with all the parts of us.

Focusing & Believing

Have you ever looked at something tiny in your hands, let's say a pebble, closed one eye and, brought it right up to your eye, and then pulled it away from your eye as far as your arm will reach? Try that right now. I'll wait. The size of the pebble doesn't change, but the perspective does. The closer our focus is on God in our lives the bigger His presence will feel. The further away He is, the less you are going to see Him. While we are on the subject of closing our one eye, let me ask maybe a silly question of you. Do you have a hard time keeping your eyes closed while in prayer? I have always been one of those lookies Lou's during prayer time. I have also been known to open my eyes while kissing, but I digress. I totally get it and understand the reverence that is shown to God through bowing my head and closing my eyes I mean, come on y'all I was raised Southern Baptist, but I say to you, there is nowhere in the Bible where God says close your eyes when you pray to me. He desires a closeness that comes from seeing you and you seeing Him. If I am having a heart to heart with someone, I cannot imagine how bad they would feel if I closed my eyes whilst talking to them or they to me. Could you?

Like the pebble, putting things into perspective is essential. Not only can you imagine that pebble as God, but now imagine that it is our main focus, assuming, of course, God is not our main focus. Maybe it's a divorce, a wayward child, death in the family, job loss, health issues, or anything else that Satan enjoys throwing at us to rock our commitment to God. As Colossians 3:2 (AMP) states, *"Set your mind and keep focused habitually on the things above {the heavenly things}, not on things that are on the earth {which have only temporal value}."* Why do we spend so much time focusing on temporal things? Just a few weeks ago, I heard my pastor speak about a stressful time in his life, and the advice he was given was spot on. I'm paraphrasing here, of course, and that is that in 20 years, it won't feel the same, it won't look the same, and your focus will be somewhere else. Now obviously, my pastor and I included preferred that the 20 years be more like 20 minutes, but it's a sliding scale, of course, depending on how much time and effort you are giving to your focus. Of course, the further away the pebble gets, the smaller the problem seems to feel. If we spend as little time as possible focusing on the things that are temporal, we will begin to change our perspective and see God up close and the worldly things at a distance. When we put things into perspective, we can focus on things like His truth, His purpose, and His love. Let us spend just a moment covering these three crucial items.

His Truth Jesus made it pretty clear when he stated in John 14:6 no matter what version you choose to read it from that, He is the way the TRUTH, and the life, and no one comes to the father accept through Him. When I think of being like Jesus, I want that kind of belief, that kind of faith, that kind of boldness that says I am a child of the highest God and no one is going to change that truth no matter how many times Satan tries to tell me different.

Another good nugget with regard to His truth is in Ephesians when Paul instructed all to wear the full armor of God, which includes the belt of truth. The belt of truth is not only the first item of the full armor but is also considered an essential ingredient to the whole armor because without it, there would be no need for the rest of the armor. Our spiritual walk with Christ can only go so far if we don't believe His truth. Throughout the Bible the Holy Spirit is also referenced as the Spirit of Truth, and though the Holy Spirit lives in us, I like to imagine that the belt of truth is the external version of the Holy Spirit. When I think of the purpose of today's belts, it isn't to protect or carry a sword; it is to hold one's pants up, which is found mostly on men with pockets full and skinnier ladies who lack the backside. Therefore, the Spirit of Truth is my helper and the wisdom I need to protect myself from exposure to things that are not of God.

His Purpose My go-to Bible verse that I would be absolutely remiss in excluding is the one I use when I do not understand His ultimate plan or even His next step. Romans

8:28 I spend a great deal of time repeating it over and over in my mind *"And we know that God causes EVERYTHING to work together for good of those who love God and are called according to His purpose for them."* What an enormous weight we can lift off our shoulders with the knowledge that it isn't something. It is EVERYTHING. We can be confident in knowing that if we focus and believe the sword of the spirit (the Bible) and that the belt of truth carries His purpose, which is our most effective defense against all evil forces that attempt to penetrate God's plan for our lives that we cannot be defeated.

His Love Do you remember your first date with your true love? Or the moment you laid eyes on your first-born child? Or any other time when you experience immense feelings within your body, known as the butterflies. Imagine that times 1000, and even that wouldn't be able to explain how wide and how deep God's love for you and I is. Agape love is what is considered the highest form of love, sacrificial love with no expectations in return. There is no greater sacrifice than watching your son die for the lives of believers and non-believers alike. During my time in Southeast Asia as a missionary, I told 100's of Buddhists the story of Jesus Christ, and at the end of my story, I showed them all a photo of my three children in a cute and funny pose, and everyone had a little chuckle. I looked at everyone with tears in my eyes and said I would never be able to allow the suffering that Jesus suffered for me and for you on any of my children. No way no when no how. Never, sorry, not sorry. To sacrifice the only sinless individual that has ever been and will ever be on this earth is not ever something comprehendible; that is what is called agape love.

These 3 things are some of the ways that have worked for me to feel God's presence in my life accepting his truth, trusting his purpose in everything, and accepting he loves ole undeserving flawed me beyond comprehension.

My Father Loves Me

When I think of agape love and the role that God plays in our lives, I try and imagine the ideal father figure. Being a product of the 80s, my example of the ideal father was none other than Michael J Fox's father in *Family Ties*. The show ran from 1982 to 1989. Steven Keaton, played by Michael Gross, was to me the wholesome father figure and would have won the who's who of pre-teen girls' dream fathers. He was kind and compassionate, funny and loving, and did not shuck his parental duties. My father was all those things as well, and though I can look back on my father as an adult and realize there were cracks growing up, I was blessed not to realize them and grateful for his influence in my life. However wonderful my father was, I realize not every one of us has had that example set before them and, therefore, felt it necessary to reference Steven Keaton. You see, though we may not have had the ideal father figure in our lives, we can still imagine the concept of one. Whether it be a TV show father, a friend's father, a teacher, or even a dad you saw on the playground running around playing with his child, we can all muster up the idea of what a perfect dad looks like to us. Now imagine having that idyllic relationship at your constant fingertips. That is what God desires for our relationship with Him. A unity between He and us that is so perfect that we no longer need to seek worldly human approval. The perfect father is within our grasp, we need only grasp that connection.

My True BFF

Maybe the concept of a perfect father isn't something that you can grasp. Maybe you were hurt so badly by the father figures in your life and cannot grapple with the concept of a perfect father. Let's try a different perspective. Relationships on earth are complex and difficult, especially for me. I will say I have a bit of loving envy for those who have had lifelong friendships. I do not have that in my life. I believe that my choices in life are to blame for the lack of long-term friendships. God and my counselor are working on that with me. I do, however, revert to the concept that I am wonderfully made in God's image and that if He wanted me to have the personality type that maintained long-term friendships, I would have it. But can you just for a moment ask yourself what the best, best friend would look like to you?

Imagine your BFF that fits you to a tee. Would they know all your flaws and love you anyways? Would they stick by you through thick and thin? Would they never leave your side even though you were undeserving and you treated them with disregard and even disrespect? Would they make themselves available to you above everything else, never saying, "Sorry, I don't have the time for you?" Would they know just the right words at the right time every time? I appeal to you that this BFF already exists. And He is presently three and one, this omni presence, seated at the right hand and dwelling within your soul. When challenged with life's difficulties, having the confidence that comes with feeling God's presence in EVERY situation can bring about a peace that passes all understanding in our gray matter.

I do not blame my parents for my personality type, but I did do a lot of moving around as a child. My father was always chasing a dream that he never seemed to achieve and was always willing to uproot us to follow the next best idea he had to set us up on an easy street. At the time of my high school diploma, which in itself was a great accomplishment, I had attended 13 different schools. As extraverted as I was and still am to this day, I wasn't necessarily given the opportunities to create lasting friendships, and in turn, I don't value them to the degree as much. I find it challenging to maintain long-term commitments to others. I did, however, have Teddy.

My stuffed animal bear, conveniently named Teddy is, was and will always be a constant reminder of my lack of an imaginary friend and my desire for connection as young as the remembered age of 5. Since my only sibling, a brother, was four and a half years younger than I was, I learned to play by myself. Teddy and I would have tea parties at my mom's prompting and make mud pies together at my prompting. The lack of communication was definitely there. Teddy did not talk back. Yes, I spoke on his behalf, and we conversed, but it was pretty one-sided. Another perspective I am offering here as if you didn't have the ideal father, never had a perfect BFF, maybe you had the quintessential imaginary friend. Just to be clear, I am not implying God is imaginary in any way, shape, or form. I do, however, believe like an imaginary friend, God is <u>always</u> there, always looking to talk to you, met your needs, and love on you like, well like Teddy.

When I think of heaven, I think of all the times I've said throughout my life "In a perfect world" to try and look at the positive side of situations. Heaven is and will be the only "perfect world." The point is that we are all such flawed human beings. We will fail others, and others will fail us. The movie *Face Off* with John Travolta and Nicholas Cage comes to mind. Spoiler alert ahead: Travolta is a cop who has his face removed and replaced with Cage's to try and get details in a maximum prison, and of course, things go south. There is a scene where Travolta, playing the bad guy, which is Cage's character, has a gun to someone's head. He squeals like a pig and says, *"Weeee we have a predicament."* We do have a predicament, don't we. Jesus did not in any way beat around the bush on this one. He made it abundantly clear when He said in John 15:12 (NLT) *"Love each other in the same way I have loved you."* YIKES!

"Whatcha talkin' about Willis?" If you get it, you get it.

Jesus loved us without sin because he was sinless. Jesus loved us without flaws because he was flawless. Jesus loved us on the cross and died for our sins, and that is His commandment to us. I say again, yikes! This predicament just gets bigger and bigger unless we seek Him first. With this realization, feeling God's presence is our goal; the assertion must be to accept that He will never leave you and will not forsake you. With the acceptance of this, the flaws of others will not hurt as much because our faith and trust are tied to the right place. He alone has got this. He knew the flawed person was going to do something that hurt you and/or I before we did. With this knowledge under our belt, we can take on the most painful experiences with the comprehension that He is present, and He's got this too.

ACTIONS

Communication is my love language. Just ask my quiet husband. Prayer is the quickest and most effective avenue I have taken in feeling God's presence in my everyday life. I talk to Him about everything, from asking Him to change the red light to green before my car comes to a stop to my deepest darkest secrets only He knows. Reverence for His mightiness is in our movement during our communication with God. Raising our hands, taking a knee, or bowing our heads. The common phrase "Actions speak louder than words" dates to a sermon by Saint Antony of Padua in 1200. However, it has been used by many of the likes such as Ben Franklin, Mark Twain, and me, and not just in this moment. If someone says they love you but don't show you that they love you, do they really love you? As I make this statement part of my belief system, I then must admit that my actions must show love as well. I can pray to God 24/7. I should be since Paul said to the Thessalonians in 1 Thessalonians 5:16 *"Never stop praying."* but truly, if my actions aren't lining up with my desires, my intentions, and my love for God, then will I really feel God's presence in my life and experience the enlightenment within my relationship with God?

Psalm 116:13 encourages us to lift up our cup of salvation and praise the Lord for saving us. A friend of mine in all her kookiness, decided to take that literally and began raising her hand up and cupping them during worship. My first thought was, "Ok my girl has gone a bit off the rails with this one," but hey, who am I to judge? Maybe she had something there. I attempted it and felt an overwhelming sense of humility and closeness to Jesus. I raised my cup in thanks, and He poured down His abundant love and comfort back into that cup. When you connect your actions to your prayers, it pleases the Lord. It is in these little actions of submission that He draws nearer, and you feel His undeniable presence.

Simple acts such as these can be a bit of a challenge for some of us control freaks who find it challenging to relinquish control. Every time, and I am not exaggerating here, every time I trusted Him, God has shown me (and not in a Biff to McFly, *"Back to the Future"* kind of tapping my head, *"Hello, hello is anybody home?"* fashion either) that His way was so much better for me, and I am blessed because of that knowledge.

There is so much more packed into our actions than our words, and if we embrace the knowledge that His will is just flat-out better for us than what we can even fathom, we will undoubtedly feel His presence. With those feelings comes a connection that allows us to see His miraculous work in and around us.

YOU

CHAPTER 9

Who Am I To Be Used

Confession

How could I be used by God? How on earth could He ever use me? Such a nobody-special, midwestern grandmother with limited resources and knowledge, not to mention a tawdry past. But here's the good news. He can. He can use you and me. We need only stand up and volunteer ourselves, sit back, and watch what Jesus does in our lives.

I am reminded of the 2012 movie Hunger Games, where Katniss Everdeen, played by Jennifer Lawerence, stood up for her younger sister and said those infamous award-winning words, "I volunteer as tribute!" Tribute refers to giving up something voluntarily in appreciation or out of gratitude. Katniss chose to take the place of her sister, and Jesus chose to take the place of you and I for our sins. Getting the connection yet? Like Katniss's sister, we owe a great deal of gratitude to Jesus for saving us, and we should all be willing to stand tall and say to God, "I volunteer as tribute for Jesus!" No matter where you are in your walk with Christ you too can be used. This was a difficult concept for me to grasp, and I hope that the words that follow help you to feel like you too can be used by God.

God had, of course, already forgiven me for my spiritual diversion years prior to my accident, but I hadn't. I felt guilty and disconnected, not remotely worthy of His forgiveness. Not worthy of His blessings. The realization that I needed God in a way I hadn't had Him in a very long time was the only way I was going to be able to get past my prior shortcomings. The pain I caused.

Why didn't I feel worthy? What was it that had plagued me so deeply? In the past, I can say I always wanted more; I was never satisfied. In early 2010, I had been married to my husband Doug for 10 years or so, we had three amazing healthy children, I was extremely active in the church. I ran a pro-life ministry, worked in children's ministry, was the event coordinator of our Sunday school, and volunteered at the local pregnancy resource center, all while making dinner and working my dream job at the time as a staff appraiser for Bank of America. I was living the American dream. House on a hill, a nice car, and good friends, but most importantly, I was a fully devoted follower of Christ, or so I thought.

The devil had other plans in mind. Though I wouldn't say my life was perfect, it was good. Though I wouldn't say I had the perfect marriage, it too was good. It is important to preface here that this can happen to anyone, and it is not something as I write this today that I have a problem dealing with or sharing because if I can help one person with my message to get out of their mess, I have done my job here. Not to mention, I AM FORGIVEN!

Social media is the route of all evil. In 2010, I found my high school sweetheart. The one that got away, he was my first everything, and I was smitten. Somehow, Satan knew just what it would take to break what I can now see was my house of cards and to shatter my very existence. As active as I was in ministry and focusing on God, I had a weakness, one I didn't even know existed and it was at that moment I began an emotional affair that later turned into two divorces. I am only human. I have made a lot of mistakes in my life and can accept this as my truth. Looking back on this I can say with the utmost certainty that God had a bigger plan for my life and that I am worthy to be here. I am supposed to be alive for God's purpose in my life. However, it has been an enormous struggle to get here. Today, it is easy to see that my actions when I left my husband, my church and a great deal of relationships was the most selfish thing I had ever done. The pain I caused the people I cared about put me in a downward spiral of self-loathing and disappointment. I did not feel worthy of God's love or especially His forgiveness. I found myself laying my errors at the altar daily and picking it back up the same day. My disconnect from everything I had been so committed to was like a searing hot poker to my heart and I fell into this pit of despair and anger. Fast forward 9 years later, it is now 2019. I had been divorced from my high school sweetheart and was living with a non-believer (Michael), setting this horrible example for my three now young adult children. At the time of my accident, I was back in a church and attending regularly. It was strangely a church plant from the church I attended with my husband Doug. Some of the members I knew from the good ole days. There were some feelings of uncomfortableness or maybe some judgment. To be completely honest, I felt deserving of those feelings and that I deserved the blow-off from some of the ladies. I had also chosen to separate from them when I had what I like to call my fall from grace. I had had it all, and with one click on Facebook, it was all gone. I allowed Satan to completely destroy everything I had worked so hard to achieve for Christ in my life and in the lives of my family members, and my testimony was shattered. But GOD!

Repentance = Forgiveness

This may resonate with you, and it may not. You might be reading this and thinking, why on earth am I nine chapters into reading and just now getting these intimate details of this lady's past? Let me sum it up for you! God can and does use anyone for anything, and He loves me; sins, mistakes, and all because of the shedding of the blood of His son Jesus Christ. I am You. I am a sinner. You are a sinner too. We are riddled with mistakes. The problem with these mistakes or sins is when we allow them to take root in our souls. When we allow Satan a foothold in our lives by succumbing to the feelings of failure and not standing up to Satan and saying enough is enough. I am a child of the Most High God, and you cannot ever take that away from me, Satan. There is a reason why the rear-view mirror that looks behind us is so small, and the windshield is so big. In driving through our lives, we need to focus on what is right in front of us and spend less time looking in the rear-view mirrors of our pasts.

There is not one of us on this planet that can be without sin. To live a sinless life is impossible. God doesn't call us to be sinless; he calls us to be as much like Jesus as possible. God forgives our sins when we repent. Hebrews 8:12 states, *"...I will forgive their wickedness, and I will never again remember their sins."* I once heard a pastor put it like this. Because of Jesus's death on the cross, God sees us through blood-stained lenses. I like to think of God up in heaven looking down on us with those cool round glasses with bright red glass that reminds you of the John Lennon look. Because Jesus was perfect and God sees us through the blood of Jesus's sacrifice, we are perfect in God's eyes.

Now, there is one caveat which is we must seek His forgiveness for our sins, and only then will He see our sins no more. Repentance is key. Accepting our shortcomings and failures and seeking God's forgiveness is the only way we can feel worthy of His blessings on us and in our lives. Through repentance, we find the strength and courage to follow God's path for our lives. Through repentance, we can truly stand before the Lord with all our failures in our past and know that He will still say, *"Well done, my good and faithful servant!"* The attaboy of all attaboys is in our grasp if we only accept our failures and seek forgiveness.

Fearing Rejection or Failure

For a very long time, I found myself putting off writing this book. Not because I don't think the story is valid or necessary to share, just out of pure fear of failure or rejection, I can only surmise. He has other plans there is no doubt. I am constantly being brought things by God to write about. My mind races with ideas and thoughts of things to write, to say, to share, but in the past, I would try so hard to almost block them out completely. I am so drawn to this that it has become a necessity to complete. I have recently considered this quandary as a positive connection to God. Something the writers of the Bible, I'm most certain, felt when God was speaking to them and putting their plight before them to share His word. I believe the stories in the Bible to be true all of them from Genesis 1:1 to Revelation 22:21. I believe the purpose is for us to relate to the stories and implement those actions taken by the wise or not so wise people of the Bible in our lives. When I begin to falter or question my abilities and the path I believe God has me on, I think of Noah and the ark. How many people must have thought of him as a raging lunatic for devoting so much of his time and energy to something only Noah could understand. Today, there is debate as to whether Noah was mocked as it is not explicitly stated within the Bible however, let's be honest, there is no way he was not. Though I have been blessed with the support of my family and friends in my endeavor to follow God's prompting in my life, I can assure you there are mockers. There are certainly people I have offended over my life that may be reading these words right now with judgement in their hearts. You know what, that is ok. Why is it ok for me to say let them judge, let them mock, you ask? Because we are all just humans, the approval I need doesn't come from people; it comes from the Lord and He alone. There comes a point where we as Christians must rise up UNASHAMED of who we are today and remember no more who we were and say I will follow you into battle without fear and without concern of failure like Noah.

Lord Liberation

To liberate is to release from oppression or to break the chains that bind. Choosing to open yourself up to be used by God is liberating beyond measure. The binding of your past or of you as a person, even today, fall off like loose-fitting clothes on a Weight Watchers commercial. The weight of those chains in your life can be gone. Whatever that weight looks like in your life, God sees our hearts better than we even do. He knows your pains, He knows your mistakes, He knows your failures, He knows it all but desires to use you to bring about goodness in His name anyway. He desires to give you that strength that can only come from what I like to call the Lord liberation.

The only way to truly receive the immeasurable feeling of dropping the weight of all your binding chains of the past is to do as David sang in Psalm 55:22: *"Give you burdens to the Lord, and he will take care of you. He will not permit the godly to slip and fall."* Jesus is the liberator overall. He is the Lord of salvation, and with Jesus at the heart of your life, you can be assured that liberation is to follow. With Jesus there is nothing out of your reach. With Jesus there is nothing you cannot do. With Jesus your possibilities are limitless. Accepting the limitless liberation from the Lord is just another amazing way God offers us to bear witness to His glorious miracles throughout our lives. I would encourage you to put this concept to a test through prayer.

Heavenly Father, I humble myself before you.
I pray that you forgive me of my past and use
it for your good. I pray that you liberate me
from the chains that bind me and bring
forth a newness in my life today.
I repent of my past and desire to serve
you and you alone until I stand before you at your
right hand. AMEN.

Jesus Courage

Satan is masterful at taking the courage we have for Christ and minimalizing it. As soon as you begin to step out for Christ, he will make you question it all. The idiom of taking one step forward and three steps back comes to mind. Progression will not always be linear in life. We will fall off the horse, but we must get back on to truly be a good rider of this one life God has given us.

How do we dust ourselves off and get back on the horse again? Mustering up the courage to face our faults, our failures, and the nay-sayers can only come from Jesus. As Jesus was walking on water during a storm that the disciples were in, they were afraid, and Jesus said in Matthew 14:27 *"Do not be afraid, take courage I am here."* He was with them then, and He is with you now.

An even larger example of Christ's courage is in His last days. Because Jesus was the son of God, He knew what His responsibility on earth was. He knew He was going to suffer unimaginable pain for our sins. In the Garden of Gethsemane, Jesus was under such a great deal of stress He was believed to suffer from a very rare condition, hematidrosis. Hematidrosis is a disorder in which one's sweat is blood-like, brought on by extreme stress on the body. Anxiety like nothing you or I can fathom is what He suffered. But when the soldiers came surrounding Him amongst olive trees known for peace and the relationship between God and His people Jesus accepted His role and said, *"Who are you looking for?"* The soldiers stated, *"Jesus the Nazarene."* This is the moment, the moment you and I would most likely find difficulty and He said, *"I am He."* When Satan tries to manipulate you into thinking you do not have what it takes or you do not have the ability to take the criticism or the shame remember those three words to find your courage *"I AM HE!"*

Choices

Imagine just for a second because this one is a doozy, and that is how many choices you make in a day. From the second you wake up to the second you fall asleep how many decisions do you make. Thousands if not hundreds of thousands of choices every day. From simple things that you do without thought to things that require a great deal of thought. Like for some of us what to wear is a big decision but what leg to put in your pants first is not. Significant decisions and not so significant decisions are constantly being made by everyone. How we think determines our choices Proverbs 4:23 (NCV) states *"Be careful what you think, because your thoughts run your life."* Because our thoughts are what run our lives it is important to make well thought out choices.

George Miller an American psychologist was one of the founders of cognitive psychology experimented with short term memory and established what is now understood as Miller's Law. This law conceptualizes the idea that your short-term memory can only hold seven items plus or minus two things at a time. Therefore, your immediate memory or what is available to you without thought. Your short-term capacity if you will retain seven binary choices at once.

Under this belief the short-term conscious choices we make to give our attention to are what define our lives. My suggestion is that one, if not more, of those seven choices always include Jesus. Dr Paul Tripp is quoted as saying, *"No one is more influential in your life than you are, because no one talks to you more than you do."* Ask yourself these things. What choices are your thoughts making for you in your life? Is at least one of your seven thoughts on Jesus? If not, how can you make better choices in your life to always have your thoughts pointing you in the direction God wants for you and your life?

Oops!... I did it again!

Yes, I will admit I like Brittany Spear's music from time to time. I am a crazy dancer while I am driving in the car kind of lady, and her poppy boppy music can really get my hips moving and arms flailing.

> *Oops, I did it again*
> *I played with your heart, got lost in the game*
> *Oh baby, baby*
> *Oops, you think I'm in love*
> *That I'm sent from above*
> *I'm not that innocent.*

We are all like Brittany in that we are not that innocent. We all have an innate sinful nature. To a degree, this nature is out of our control. In Romans 3, Paul makes it explicitly clear that no one can obey the law perfectly and that we all deserve to be deemed unrighteous for our sinfulness. Alas, there is a solution to our sinful nature, and that is knowing that not only is our sin forgiven when we repent, but God can use our sins for His good. That gives me an undeniable hope that our imperfections are God's design as well. He knows we aren't going to be perfect. Hallelujah!! To me, there is something so beautiful in knowing that as long as I am striving every day to be as much like Jesus as possible, God can use my failures to bring about change and use my not-so-Jesus moments for Jesus. This thinking is something that can ultimately bring contentment to your heart and soul. Having this thought process can bring about great change in how you view your contribution to Christ. None of us are worthy, but by His grace, we are all worthy, and because you and I are chosen to be here at this time, it is our duty to be who He created us to be in His image. Do I always stand in front of the mirror and see who God sees I'd be remiss in saying yes. But captivating that as quickly as I can helps us to know it as lies from Satan. No matter how many times you Oops.... again and again, God never stops loving you and wanting you to be all that He has planned for you in this life and for eternity.

Blips & Dust

A blip is defined as something temporary that is relatively small, inconsequential within a larger context. Typically, a blip is considered a hiccup or mistake. However, a blip in time can be explained as a blink of the eye, a quick moment overall. Because God sees everything in the grand scheme, we can be considered a blip in the overall picture of the universe from beginning to end.

A friend of mine references a lot of things as dust in the wind. She points out how terribly irrelevant things are in life, and that we tend to make big deals when they really are just a speck in the bigger picture. It seems silly to sometimes think of the things that she and I have discussed over the years that have upset us or frustrated us when those things are really so truly overall insignificant.

Though we are both blips and dust in the wind in God's great plan, we are significant to Him. Every action we take, every choice we make He cares. He cares about you and me, the guy who cuts you off on the way to work or the boss who makes you feel inferior. He cares about each and every one of us so much that He gave His ONLY son for your life, and though you may be thinking I don't know my purpose, I can guarantee God does. You need only ask Him to use you.

Our time here on earth is written, and it is small in the concept of God's overall plan. What shall you do with the time you have left? Will you continue looking at life through the concave view of a magnifying lens or will you start seeing the opportunities God places in front of you as opportunities to bless others and be used by God for His good no matter what you see in the mirror? Will you accept your mess as your message and choose to be used by God with all your flaws and all your tawdry past? You need only be open to seeing all of it as your personal tools unlike anyone else He has created. If God can use my mess He can and will use yours.

CHAPTER 10

Awaken Your Soul

"Wake Up Little Susie"

In 1958, the Everly Brothers released the song "Wake Up Little Susie," One of the most controversial songs for its time, so much so that the Catholic archbishop had it banned from Boston radio, stating it was too suggestive. The song was the catalyst for their career, topping the charts at number one, and later in life, it was attributed to their induction into the Rock & Roll Hall of Fame and Country Hall of Fame as well as a Grammy Lifetime Achievement award. I personally used to hear it on a 45' record while my dad played the drums to it, and my mother and I danced around the living room. My how the times have changed 65 years later; we are fighting evil and corruption on an unfathomable level. It is time we WAKE UP! It is time we as Christians stop sitting in the pew singing on Sunday and letting the corrupt worldview run our lives the other 6 days of the week.

Like little Susie our reputation is shot, and we as fully devoted followers of Christ must step out of our comfort zones and start making our voices heard and change the trajectory of our lives. We must open our eyes to everything going on around us and stop hiding in our comfort zones if we truly want to experience all that God has to offer us.

Some practical ways to start to get out of your comfort zone include but are not limited to. Reading the parts of the Bible that encourage you to be courageous and share your truth. One of my favorite verses that has me continuing to write is this.

*But my life is worth nothing to me unless
I use it for finishing the work assigned me by
the Lord Jesus- the work of telling others
the Good News about the wonderful grace of God.
Acts 20:24*

Another practical application in your life is to be aware of your surroundings. It is extremely easy to get comfortable with just not knowing what is happening. There is peace that comes with ignorance. Thus, the saying "Ignorance is bliss!" We are not supposed to sit by idly and let our surroundings suffer. Paul encourages us in 1 Timothy 6:12 *Fight the good fight for true faith.* Because Jesus came and died for you and for me, we do not have to fight like warriors of the Old Testament, but we are supposed to be true to His word all of it and not turn a blind eye in acceptance of the world around us that is full of sin. We were spiritual blind as Jesus indicated in John 9:35-41, but we are no longer because He has opened our eyes. Our eyes now see what is true and good. He desires us to make an impact in this world not just on our couch seats.

Catch A Fire

Stop doing what is easy for Christ and catch fire for Christ. My son Brayden has always been into music; it has always been a source of comfort and solace for him. Toby Mac's song *"Catch A Fire'* is a song that brings about genuine joy in my soul when I hear it. It takes me back to a time when Brayden was young, impressionable, and full of fire for Christ. We would crank it up as loud as we could and scream it at the top of our lungs.

*Whoopsie-daisy, call me crazy, whoopsie-daisy
Come, we gonna catch that
Fire.....*

I realize music isn't necessarily something that everyone uses to get emotionally charged for Christ, but there is a reason every church service starts with a tune. It may be the words, it may be the hymn or it may be the emotions that invoke the will to draw nearer to God. For me, it is absolutely all of it. My body becomes one with my desires when I sing my heart out for Christ. Even in the car with my then 12-year-old to today, there is something about music that just gets me fired up for Jesus. What is it that fires you up for Christ? What is it that one thing that brings joy to your soul? Whatever that one thing is for you, it is important to use it daily and in times of disconnection. Satan will always try his best to disconnect you from your source, and without it, you will fizzle. Enthusiasm is key to feeling, seeing, and experiencing miracles. Without catching the fire and keeping the embers burning, Satan will infiltrate your life. God does not favor us when we fizzle. Complacency is easy to allow into your relationship with God because Satan is working hard through the world, and the things you may be thinking are important. To experience the awakening of your soul that opens you up requires a great deal of the opposite of complacency.

It is best described by Dr. Benjamin E Mays, a Baptist minister known for his civil rights activism, who is quoted as saying, *"The tragedy of life is often not in our failures, but rather in our complacency, not in our doing too much, rather in our doing too little; not in our living above our ability, but rather in our living below our capacities."* God desires you to focus on your fire and not your fizzle.

If you don't know what your fire starter is, pray this short prayer for God to open your eyes to what starts your fire for him.

Father, I humble myself before you
with a heart to serve you and you alone.
Open my eyes to the areas I am complacent
and bring about a fire in me. A fire that
is unique to me alone because only you
know me better than myself. Amen.

Life's Playbook

Playbooks are used in a variety of ways. Businesses, sports, marketing, sales, software, and even cyber security and software to name only a few. They are designed to enlighten and educate in that field. Ultimately, it inspires knowledge on how to become more effective in that genre. Hands down, the most effective way to better understand how to awaken your soul to the glory of miracles and knowledge of the blessings God desires for you and your life is through the Bible. This is number one. If you take nothing away from reading my words other than this, I have followed God's prompting in writing these words to you. The Bible is, without a doubt, the best playbook for life. Taking time on a daily basis to read His word is and will always be instrumental in opening yourself up to all that a relationship with God has to offer.

There are 66 books, 1189 chapters, and 31,102 verses in the Bible. Sometimes, picking up the Bible can be daunting, almost overwhelming, because there is so much to unpack in its pages. Like most playbooks, there are ways to decipher information that you are looking to educate yourself on. To go deeper and grow closer to God through His word, having a life application study Bible can go a long way. It's the Super Bowl playbook, if you will.

The life application study bible is specifically designed to empower you with the tools to apply and educate you on how to apply the Bible's teaching in your daily life. It has extensive cross-references to help you locate similar concepts throughout the Bible. It additionally has a master index, which has everything from obscure names you hear only once to hot topics of today. I am a bit of a lover of history, and something else that is helpful is the key places within the chapters is mapped out in order for you the reader to see exactly where the story took place.

In a world where everything is only a click away, it is easy to just google verses, and I find myself looking for the easier way from time to time. It is okay to do this from time to time. However, it should not be your number one choice for your source. There is just something about taking the time to find your answers vs. just getting the information from the internet. When you utilize digital media, it lacks the memorability of the search. When something is convenient it's also easily forgotten. Not to mention what usually happens to me because the internet offers so much data Satan tends to sidetrack my thinking, and before I know it, I am reading how to build a bomb shelter in my backyard, and I've forgotten why I got on the internet, to begin with. When you physically take the time to search for something for a reference, you're more likely to have a more profound retention of the knowledge you gained from researching the topic.

With this tool God has perfectly provided your opening to miracles and to your relationship with God is only pages away.

Runner Up

In close second to the Bible is none other than prayer. Some people are prayer warriors who talk to God all the time about anything and everything. Some people pray once a day. Some people pray only when life is getting rough and they feel like they need help. Some people only pray for others and not themselves. However, you choose to pray, and whenever you pray, I do not sit in a place of judgement over your choices. I do want to share with you how much prayer can change your life. Like anything, the more you do something, the better you get at it. Paul made it as clear and clear as can be in 1 Thessalonians 5:17 when he instructed the Thessalonians to *"Never stop praying."* Where your thoughts are, so is your heart. The more time you spend in prayer with God, the closer you will become to him; it doesn't get more simpler than this. To truly see his workings in and around you, it boils down to simply having that deeper connection to Christ. The more you share with Him, the more He will reveal to you.

Double Down

Doubt in yourself and your convictions may come. Satan takes great pleasure in creating doubt. Those feelings of not being good enough, not knowing enough, not deserving it are all from Satan. God does not give us a doubtful heart; Satan does. It is in those times you are best to double down and seek wise counsel. Doubling down is, of course, an action that might seem risky. Almost uncomfortable because you might feel vulnerable and uncertain. Doubling down is, of course, synonymous with card games. It shows the strengthening of your commitment to other players. Other players in this explanation are, first and foremost, yourself as a player, other Christians, non-Christians, of course, God, and, pretty much anyone in your sphere of influence. The best way to overcome feelings of uncertainty is to seek counsel from others. Proverbs 12:15 encourages us to seek counsel *"Fools think their own way is right, but the wise listen to others."* This is not something that comes easily to me. I find myself not liking to admit where I fall short. I know, I know, that doesn't make a lot of sense as you are nearing the end of this book and my sharing of my shame. Here is why I believe that to truly awaken your soul, you need to not try bluffing your way through those times of doubt. Bluffing is also a card game technique that requires deceiving the other players into thinking you have a good hand when you do not really have one. It is based on deceit. The hard-core truth is if we bluff our way through life acting one way and truly feeling another, we are deceiving only ourselves. Because God knows the truth, and other people's judgements and opinions do not matter. We are robbing ourselves of the magnitude of blessings God has to show us in our lifetime.

When we seek wise counsel, we grow. We grow closer to God, we grow closer to the counselor, and we grow as Christians. Wise counsel can come from a magnitude of directions, but ultimately it is in your best interest to find the counsel you feel most comfortable with sharing your doubts. Always remember other people make mistakes, that is why you want to seek wise counsel, not just any counsel. And, if you don't agree with the counsel, don't abandon your love for God because of someone else who professes to be His follower because we are all human, even the wise. My suggestion would be to always accept the counsel graciously and then make sure to back it up with God's scripture.

Be Bold

No matter whether you are an introvert or extravert, you can be bold for Christ. Extraverts are known for their boldness; however, many would describe those with an introverted personality type as quite the opposite of bold. Another defining characteristic of introverts is humbleness. In Numbers 12:3, Moses is defined as the humblest person, more than anyone on earth. Did you get that, Moses. Moses, the guy who led the Israelites out of slavery, parted the Red Sea, wrote the Ten Commandments!

Yes, that guy was an introvert. Boldness doesn't have to come from you when you have Christ living in you. Let Jesus be your boldness to awaken your soul. I am not suggesting you talk to a burning bush, though who am I to judge. I am suggesting in order to really be awake in Christ is to find a way to be bold for Him. He who is in you can and will do miraculous things if you just step out and be as bold as a lion or lioness. Lions and lionesses are known for courage. For those of you who remember *Wizard of Oz* the lion didn't have courage, which was unusual for a lion. They are innately bold. King of the Jungle, everyone knows that thanks to Simba in *Lion King*. You don't get that title without being bold, that's for sure.

I recently took away a good nugget from Lisa Bevere, author of *"Lioness Uprising"*. She encouraged me at a conference to not allow myself to be intimidated. She shared a verse that was very valuable and has helped to keep me focused. I pray that the next verses encourage you to be bold and courageous for Christ as it has been for me.

> *Don't be afraid.......*
> *For the time is coming when everything*
> *that is covered will be revealed,*
> *and all that is secret will be made known to all.*
> *What I tell you now in darkness,*
> *shout abroad when daybreak comes.*
> *What I whisper in your ear,*
> *shout from the rooftops for all to hear.*
> *Matthew 10:26-27*

Be a Doer

One of my favorite actors is Mark Wahlberg. He has stayed true to his faith in the face of Hollywood adversity. Besides that, I think he's an awesome actor. A movie that just cracks me up is *"Pain and Gain"*. In this movie, Wahlberg plays Daniel Lugo, a bodybuilder turned criminal. Though his concept of how to go about being a doer was obviously flawed, he had the right idea. We all should be doers for God. Being a doer just means we should all do our part. The church (His people) are the living body to the head (Jesus Christ). We are called to serve. We are called to show God's love through our actions. As the body, we are representatives of Jesus. It is necessary that we get out of the church pews and be doers. Our actions should be representative of Jesus's love.

Acts of service is a love language that many people consider one of their top needs. The well-known chapter in 1 Corinthians, dubbed the love chapter, says it best, that no matter what happens, three things will remain forever, faith, hope, and love and the greatest is love. Being a doer for God is showing love. Serving others is a great way to awaken your soul to experience miracles.

Proud Papa

Being spiritually awake implies that you have reached a higher level of consciousness. Awakening your soul creates a shift in your perspective. Your ultimate goal is to see all things from a biblical perspective and not have a worldly view of things. Once you have accepted Jesus as your savior, nothing brings God more joy than when you connect your actions with your beliefs.

Imagine if you will a time in your life when you did something that made someone proud of you, and they shared that with you. Do you remember how amazing that made you feel? Can you fathom having that feeling on a daily basis because it is available to you? When you serve others and choose love, this makes God proud of you, His beloved.

Target Audience

I have heard this saying over and over from social media to the pulpit. Spoken first by Will Rogers, a humorous commentator in the early 1900's and that is *"Too many people spend money they don't have to buy things they don't need to impress people they don't like."* This statement still stands true nearly 100 years later. Why do we spend so much of our time and talent trying to impress the wrong target audience? The audience you need to start impressing is just an audience of one. God. When you devote more of your time to impressing God instead of people, you will quickly begin to feel and see God at work in everything that you do and say.

So just stop it, just stop caring about what everyone thinks right. Ha, what a loaded statement; why is it easy to preach this but hard to do it. There are several reasons why we spend so much time seeking approval in the wrong place. Approval is, at its core, the act of acceptance, and let's face it, who doesn't like to be accepted? One reason we devote so much time looking to be accepted by others is a lack of self-worth. But more importantly, than even lacking self-worth, I believe that because we live in a world that encourages fast gratification, we look for approval in the wrong places. Ultimately, we are all going to fail someone in our lives. I cannot begin to list the numerous people whom I have failed over my lifetime. To be frank, I shudder at the thought. When you come to the realization that has taken me a really long time to realize, and that is that the only one I need to impress is God, it is like a jaw-dropping epiphany. As long as you know your heart is in the right place, you do not need man's approval. In order to live a life pleasing to God and to come to a place of peace without worry of others opinions you must begin to focus on the purpose God has for you in your life.

Following the Plan

Imagine if God informed you today that you were to succeed His chosen one. Someone of great value to God, someone who performed miracles, someone who God spoke to in ways you never could imagine. Imagine for a hot second you are Joshua, and you have to do something greater than delivering God's people out of slavery, like bringing them into the promised land. Moses had some really big shoes to fill, and Joshua his assistant, was tasked after Moses' death to bring the Israelites into the land. Land that is being fought over to this day. Jericho Israel, is one of the oldest continually inhabited cities in the world to date. And the assistant was given the job. How much boldness and courage do you think that took to follow that plan? I can only imagine.

God made it exceedingly clear that Joshua was the one to lead the people. In Joshua 1:6-8 He not only pumped up Joshua with courage, He instructed him in a way we as believers should take notice. When you are feeling lesser than others and struggling with understanding His plan, remember these words. God spoke to Joshua and said, *"Be careful to obey instructions... Do not deviate from them, turning either to the right or the left. Then, you will be successful in everything you do. Study the book of instruction continually, meditate on it day and night so you will be sure to obey everything written in it. Only then will you prosper and succeed in all you do."*

Ok, first of all, WOW! Second, there are some things I'd like to unpack from those verses with you. I spend a lot of time focusing on the wrong things, things out of my control. Do you? If the answer is yes, this is for you. STOP!!! Look in one direction only don't worry about the left or the right; look straight ahead at the only guide you need. It begs to reason that Joshua was a wee bit concerned with the left and right. What others were going to be saying and doing, and how he was going to succeed someone so great as Moses had to be on his mind A LOT! God said just chill in my instruction, and you will succeed.

Next point, He didn't say you would succeed in some things, He didn't say you would succeed in the things in your control only, He said Joshua would succeed in EVERYTHING. In a world where success is measured by how much we have and how many likes or retweets we have, we can lose sight of what is fundamentally more important, and that is simply put here to Joshua. Just stay the course, don't deviate, and trust that EVERYTHING is in the hands of the one who desires your success over everyone else, including you. We need only follow

His plan which will in turn awaken our soul in ways unimaginable.

CHAPTER 11

CALL TO ACTION!!!

Preparedness

I recently heard a story of a faith filled women who was planning for the future in what some might consider an unconventional way. She was creating a hearty garden on her property. She was stockpiling necessities in her home. She was also praying over every bit of her property daily from the floors to the ceilings and everything in between. When asked why she was doing this didn't she have faith that God would provide for her in the end of times her response was priceless. She said "I am not doing it for myself I know where I will be. I am preparing this property for those that come here to seek refuge once I have already meet Jesus in the air and transcended to heaven."

My question to you is do you feel prepared for what is coming? Obviously, this woman is preparing for a *Left Behind* book series; Revelations end of times dooms day cataclysmic event. Personally, I think her plight is compassionate and kind and gives me a bit of hope for humanity. Hope that there are still people out that who care enough about those who didn't accept the message of the way, the truth and light being Jesus and Jesus alone that they do their part whilst still here on earth.

Historically, though, over the last century, every generation looks at what is in front of them and predicts the end of times is near. Near to you and I, and near to God, are most likely not identical, in fact, they are probably light years apart. FYI, I googled the actual distance of a light year, and it is nearly 6 trillion miles away. As Christians, we know that God is returning, whether it is in your lifetime or mine; it remains to be seen; however, there is continuous data showing the likelihood that we are living at the end of times and Jesus's return is rapidly approaching.

If the data is correct, are you prepared? Do you know with 100% certainty where you will stand on judgement day? If you are the least bit shy of 100%, please consider getting on your knees right now and praying this short prayer. Your life matters to Christ and He desires your preparedness.

Father, forgive me I am a sinner, I desire to live the rest of my days preparing myself for your return. Come into my heart, fill me with your Holy Spirit 100% now and always.
Amen

If you prayed that prayer with a penitent heart, Hallelujah! You have taken the first and most important step into preparedness. Now go grow your garden and be open to all that God desires to show you.

Rise Up

Rising up can be defined as working hard to succeed in a difficult situation. Taking the high road over Satan if you will. Jesus assured us in Luke 10:19 something so indispensable we should feel like we are warriors. He said, *"I have given you the authority over all the power of the enemy, and you can walk among snakes and scorpions and crush them."* Obviously, we are going to want to avoid actual snakes and scorpions, but metaphorically, what snakes and scorpions can you attribute to your lack of rising up? Are your snakes fear or worry? Are your scorpion's pride or greed? Determining what is holding you back from realizing the strength and destiny that Jesus has assured you is pivotal for being open to all that God has to show you. Be reminded of the old hymn written nearly 200 years ago by Pastor Edward Mote, *"My Hope is Built on Nothing Less."* Stand firm on Christ, the solid rock, because all other ground in sinking sand. This song brings about a sense of hope and assurance to one's heart that no matter the situation, standing with Jesus and the authority He has given you is better than standing with anything else.

Rising up is a call to action and in some ways it is considered standing up against injustice and a tyrannical oppressor. That is not what I am talking about here. The rise up I am encouraging is within your soul. Rise up to be the individual God created you to be. Rise up from the deceptive place Satan has you stuck and take control of the time you have on this earth to do what is right, good and just. C.S, Lewis has been quoted as saying *"You can't go back and change the beginning, but you can start where you are and change the ending."* Make that change today in your life in order to experience everything from a new perspective with and open heart and mind to all God has to offer you in this life.

PRIORITIES

This section might sting a bit for some of us, but it is necessary to say so here goes. What are your priorities? We all have the same 24 hours in a day. Jesus teaches us about money in Matthew 6:21 He makes it blatantly clear that where are treasures are so our hearts is there too. There is nothing more valuable than time. You can get back money, you can get back jobs, relationships, cars, all the stuff. You can't get back time. So, when I ask what is your priorities I am asking you what do you spend your most valuable commodity, time on?

I love pithy quotes; they make me feel more cerebral. One that comes to mind in regard to this topic is by motivational speaker Michael Altshuler. I think he said it best with, *"The bad news is time flies; the good news is you're the pilot."* Here is one more than speaks to me from William Penn, the founder of the Providence of Pennsylvania, in his book *"Some Fruits of*

Solitude" that was originally published in 1693; *time is what we want most, but, what, alas! we use worst; and for which God will certainly most strictly reckon with us, when time shall be no more."*

I believe way too many of us Christians spend too much time on things of this world and do not focus our priorities in the right direction. The direction of the son, not the sun. The light that comes from the son of man will always shine brighter in your life when you focus your attention on Him; when you turn your attention and prioritize your life with Jesus at the center, everything else pails in comparison. All the things that you once considered important and necessary just lose their luster. This is not to say being gluttonous is acceptable. There is a fine line between gluttony and greed. I am talking about a legacy for your children and your children's children and the importance of this. But truly ask yourself what kind of legacy do you really want to leave for your descendants? I am reminded of a pastor in my past sharing a story of his standing at the bedside of a old dying man and the man's words stung like a hot poker when he said "I'd do it all differently, I'd spend less time on stuff and more on people." I do not know where you are in life whether you are reading this at 10 or 100, but stop wasting another second of however long you have in this life and choose to prioritize your relationship with Jesus and leave a legacy for your people that they and you both can be proud of.

Sunday Christians

Do you go to church on Sunday after hitting the bars on Saturday? Are you living your life one foot in church and one in the world? To many of Christians are content with doing their once-a-week duty. One a week feeling like you're closer to Jesus than ever? If that is where you are, I understand I am not judging you. I have been there. Because I have been there, I feel compelled to share with you that God loves you right where you are, and He is thrilled to have you in His house on Sunday. Here comes the caveat... DO NOT STAY THERE! Like everything, we must evolve and expand ourselves to become stronger and more knowledgeable in something. Get out of the pews for Jesus, share love for Jesus with others. Start small. I am not suggesting you become a preacher or evangelist necessarily though that would be awesome. I am suggesting you do something one day of that week that is just a Jesus moment for you. Whether it be offering to pray for someone, sharing a bible verse with someone, giving of your time for someone in need. The Bible is riddled with stories of how Jesus did those things for others. He encourages us in Matthew 25:40 when he says, *"I tell you the truth, when you did it to one of the least of these, my brothers and sisters, you were doing it to me!"* It doesn't have to be much for you to begin to see the manifestation of the fruits of your kindness in your life.

Here is something I did to get more connected with Christ, and maybe it will help you in getting out of the pews. I picked a day, just one day. On that day, let's say Wednesday, because it's hump day and you are halfway through your week, be super diligent in trying not to sin. I know that seems silly because we should all try not to sin every day, right? But let me assure you it is not. When you bring it to your consciousness for one whole day, you will become hypersensitive to every little thing you do. Those days, I found myself nicer, more patient and closer to Jesus so much that I now have it on my conscious daily. You can too, just get out of the pew for Jesus.

It's all about You.... NOT!

We live in a society that pushes self-centeredness like a drug. From everything like music, movies, make-up, the nicest car, and a more updated house than the Joneses the list could go on and on. Not to mention, everywhere you turn on social media, you see AI versions of people with their fake filters to make them feel better about themselves. It can get exhausting to watch people obsess about themselves because, contrary to popular belief, it is not about you! Good news.... I know what it is about, and I am happy to share with you it is about God's ultimate plan. It is all about God's plan, the question you must ask yourself: how much you want to be a part of the ultimate plan God has for you, His beloved. Stop putting so much time and effort into the things that hold no value. This is not to say be meek and wear burkas (not that you can't if you want to of course) but it is to say don't prioritize yourself over Jesus Christ. Plain and simple as that. The order of what is important to you is what is important to God. This action of submission is not easily done, and I struggle with this more than I care to admit some days.

I recently made a list of things I needed to accomplish and shared the list with my husband. I included things that he also needed to get done and though he has been helpful with completing the list I struggle with the choices he has made on the list whilst I prefer, he do the things on the list that are important to me he has chosen the ones that he prefers to complete. This in no way is to being shared to shame my husband. I believe if the tables were turned, I would do the exact same thing almost unknowingly because we as humans are conditioned by sin in our lives to focus on what we want not what the other person desires. It is important as Christians for us to make efforts to prioritize showing God's love over our selfish desires. Just need to derail here for a quick second and say "Thank you Michael for helping me with my list. You are my hero!"

YOLO

For those of you who don't text a great deal you may not know that YOLO is an abbreviation for "You Only Live Once." There are many unique texting abbreviations. However, this aphorism caught on and became trendy in a big way in the early 2000s. It was used by teens and adults alike. When they did something stupid or dumb, they would quickly follow up with YOLO. It is true you only have one life here on earth however, our life is not a journey, it is a gift given by God. As Christians, we are supposed to be living every day for the reward which is not this life at all. It is the eternity that we have in heaven.

Living a life well lived for Jesus starts with getting out of your routine. Find ways to break out of the same ole same ole. Choose to create simple changes in your life that are doable to establish the changes. According to the National Library of Medicine the idea that it takes 21 days to create a habit is actually a myth. At a minimum it takes 66 days to create a habit after the first daily performance. It is better to presume 10 weeks instead of 3 to reach a behavior that comes naturally. With this knowledge, it should be encouraging to know that all those times you tried something for 21 days and it didn't stick, it wasn't your fault. It sure gave me a new sense of hope. Don't be hard on yourself if the habit doesn't stick just don't give up. There are few things more rewarding than actually seeing something completely followed through on.

Be the Resistance

No matter how difficult things seem in life there is always someone who suffers more than you. Someone who has it worse than you. I am not telling you that as if it is a positive, it most certainly isn't. I share that with you because it is important for us to defy what society tells us is our destiny. Your destiny is not your circumstances. Your destiny is not what other people think is your destiny. Your destiny is in your relationship with Jesus Christ. Realizing that relationship is above all others is how you fight the battle Satan wages against you. There is no doubt that when you choose your relationship with Jesus than that with the world, you will be waging war against Satan. He will begin to throw everything at you he can to sidetrack your growth, and this is the one time in your life that defiance is a must. 1 Peter 5:8-9 are truly one of my all-time favorite verses. *"Be sober-minded; be watchful. Your adversary the devil prowls around like a roaring lion, seeking someone to devour. Stand firm against him and be strong in your faith. Remember that your family of believers all over the world is going through the same kind of suffering as you are."* I don't know if it is the slight cause of oppositional defiance disorder I possess or what, but those verses give a sense of resistance like no other. I get a burning sensation in my body, and I just want to defy anything that remotely resembles anything that could pull me away from my relationship with Jesus. We are God's resistance; as Christians we are fighting the good fight for what is biblical truth. Sometimes that doesn't always reveal itself like a lion. Lions pick off the weak and struggling animals. We cannot be weaklings for Jesus, or we will not be able to stand up against the schemes of Satan. Your destiny is to defy the devil and not live a life under the condemnation that he tries to put on you. BE THE RESISTENCE.

Get Your Gold Star

Receiving a gold star in grade school deserved a celebratory dinner at my house when I was kid. Maybe it was because it was a rare occasion, I don't know. It was a sign of achieving something great that day if your teacher gave you a gold star. If you had some problems that day, you may get a silver star, if you were a real pain in the butt, you would get a blue star, and if you should have just stayed home that day you wouldn't get a star at all you would get a frowny face. I was not a bad student, but talking too much was always something that made getting that gold star a rare occurrence.

The origin of the gold star symbolism began during World War I. Any family with a family member serving proudly displayed a flag that had a blue star on it. If the family member was killed in action, the blue star flag was replaced with a gold star flag. It symbolizes heroism and outstanding achievement. Many today don't know of this honoring tradition because the flags lost their validity during the Vietnam War due to the unpopularity of that war.

Imagine the star of Bethlehem that directed the wise men to Jesus as that symbol from God that he, too had given and sacrificed His family member, His only son, for a war. A war that had been waged against the forces of darkness. Jesus fought an unbelievable fight against Satan. He fought Satan and won in every case of demonic possession. He fought Satan and won in the Judean wilderness when Satan tried tempting him. He fought Satan and won when he died on the cross and was resurrected.

As Christians we should be striving for our gold star as Satan continues to wage war against our beliefs. As Christians we need to stand firm in our commitment to God and not be afraid of speaking the truth of the eternal life that can only come by the grace of God through His son Jesus Christ. If you believe Jesus died for your sins and you have accepted Him into your heart, allowing the Holy Spirit to dwell within you then by God you better step up and start fighting like Jesus did. Paul motivates us in 1 Peter 3:14-16 when he wrote *"...even if you suffer for doing what is right God will reward you for it. So don't worry or be afraid of their threats. Instead, you must worship Christ as Lord of your life. And if someone asks you about your hope as a believer, always be ready to explain it."* Peace comes with knowing no matter how bad things might get that you are on the winning side of this war. But we must not stand by idly, we must stand firm in our convictions. Ask yourself are you truly an example of Jesus in your life? When others describe you would they give you a gold star for Jesus?

In the End

Upon our death we will stand before God in judgement over our actions here on earth. Hebrews 9:27 states *"And just as each person is destined to die once and after that comes judgement."* There was a period in my life when the fear of God was so strong it made it easier to turn my back on Him than to try to live a life pleasing to Him. My understanding was skewed and faulty. Those concerns of judgement for my actions were flat-out wrong because if I have repented of those sins, then that isn't the judgement the author of Hebrews is speaking of. God has forgiven and forgotten those actions of my past, and every time I repent and seek His forgiveness and start fresh with a heart to not continue that sin, God will not judge me for those actions. The judgement we will receive upon our death is the opposite. It is judgement for our lack of action. Lack of action looks like complacency and self-centeredness. We need only be open to acting as the Bible directs us and listening and obeying the prompting of the Holy Spirit. Choose to act for Jesus so when your time here on earth comes to an end, you will hear the words that will bring joy to your soul. *"Well done my good and faithful servant."*

Purpose

In all honesty I cannot begin to express in words the emotions I have writing this very last section of this book. This section though the last is the very most important to God. You. Tears of joy fill my eyes with the hope that this book has encouraged you as you have read it as much as it has for me in writing it. My purpose in writing this book has always been to be able to share my story as far and as wide as God allows. Let me leave you with this one last question. What is your story and how can you respond to His call to action?

aea 7/14/2024

References

ABC News, 20December 2012, "Young Adults Tweet #YOLO When They Don't Study, Get Drunk or Drive Too", https://abcnews.go.com/Health/young-adults-tweet-yolo-live-engaged-reckless-behavior/story?id=18027279

Altshuler, Michael, Goodreads, https://www.goodreads.com/quotes/144299-the-bad-news-is-time-flies-the-good-news-is

Artist Biography, "Everly Brothers", The Ed Sullivan Show, https://www.edsullivan.com/artists/the-everly-brothers/

Bricker, Sophia, "What Is the Origin of the Phrase "What would Jesus Do?", 29 December 2021, Christianity.com, https://www.christianity.com/wiki/christian-terms/what-is-the-origin-of-the-phrase-what-would-jesus-do.html

Gardner, Benjamin, December 2012, British Journal of General Practice, "Making Health Habitual: the psychology of 'habit formation' and general practice", https://www.ncbi.nlm.nih.gov/pmc/articles/PMC3505409/#:~:text=Therefore%2C%20it%20may%20be%20helpful,motivation%20until%20the%20habit%20forms.

Frost, Robert, "The Road Not Taken", Poetry Foundation, https://www.poetryfoundation.org/poems/44272/the-road-not-taken

Markham, Devon, "Incredible Miracle Maui church unscathed by fire", 15 August 2023, News Nation, https://www.newsnationnow.com/religion/incredible-miracle-maui-church-unscathed-fire/

Mays, Benjamin, Brainy Quotes, https://www.brainyquote.com/quotes/benjamin_e_mays_610662

Mckinney,Russell,17December2018"The Disciple's Road" https://russellmckinney.com/2018/12/17/gods-gold-star/

Mote Edward, "My Hope is Built on Nothing Less Hymn Story", Phamox Music, https://phamoxmusic.com/my-hope-is-built-on-nothing-less/#google_vignette

Niles, Billy, "Dead for an Hour and Lived to Tell the Tale: The Miraculous True Story Behind Breakthrough",ENews,17August2019 https://www.eonline.com/news/1033103/dead-for-an-hour-and-lived-to-tell-the-tale-the-miraculous-true-story-behind-breakthrough

Pope, Charles "What were weddings like in Jesus Day" Catholic Standard, 1 August 2019, https://cathstan.org/posts/what-were-weddings-like-in-jesus-day-2

Rogers, Will, Good Reads, https://www.goodreads.com/quotes/238077-too-many-people-spend-money-they-haven-t-earned-to-uy#:~:text=Quote%20by%20Will%20Rogers%3A%20%E2%80%9CToo,%27t%20earned...%E2%80%9D

Savchuk, Vlad, "Demon Slayers: Isaiah Saldivar & Vlad Savchuk Interview" On Point w/ Pastor Greg Locke, 14 December 2022, https://lockemedia.org/video/demon-slayers-isaiah-saldivar-vlad-savchuk-interview-on-point-w-pastor-greg-locke/

White, Kimberly "Widower Runs Into Man Who Caused Accident That Killed Wife & Chooses Forgiveness", 27 December 2018, Inspire More, https://www.inspiremore.com/erik-fitzgerald-forgives-matt-swatzell/u

Winnemucca, Sarah, "Today in History -October 14", Library of Congress, https://www.loc.gov/item/today-in-history/october-14/#:~:text=Time%20is%20what%20we%20want,Originally%20published%201693.

All Scripture references were taken from Bible Gateway NLT unless otherwise noted.

https://www.biblegateway.com/versions/New-Living-Translation-NLT-Bible/

Holy Bible, New Living Translation, copyright © 1996, 2004, 2015 by Tyndale House Foundation. Used by permission of Tyndale House Publishers, Inc., Carol Stream, Illinois 60188. All rights reserved.

All quoted song lyrics were taken from www.lyricsmode.com.

Made in the USA
Monee, IL
22 January 2024